795

Wrap It Up!

Memorable Meeting Enders for Youth Groups

Paul Borthwick ▼ Karen Dockrey
Steve Hickey ▼ Mark Oestreicher
Sue Reck ▼ Tim Richards

David C. Cook Publishing Co., Elgin, Illinois——Weston, Ontario

Here's a collection of over 100 new ideas to help you create incredible meetings. Use these activities to plug into your existing curriculum when it calls for something you know won't work with your group. Or, pick and choose from several ideas in this series to create entire meetings from scratch. Use these ideas for Junior High/Middle School or High School. Use them for youth group or Sunday school. Just don't use them all at once! We'd love to hear how you were able to use these activities—and we're always open to hearing new ideas that you come up with. We'll pay you for any we end up using. Write to us at the address below. Now get to work, and have an incredibly good time!

Incredible Meeting Makers
Wrap It Up!

© 1993 David C. Cook Publishing Co.

Unless otherwise noted, Scripture quotations are from the Holy Bible, New International Version (NIV), © 1973, 1978, 1984 by International Bible Society. Used by permission of Zondervan Bible Publishers.

Published by David C. Cook Publishing Co.
850 North Grove Ave., Elgin, IL 60120
Cable address: DCCOOK
Series editor: Randy Southern
Editor: Sharon Stultz
Additional ideas provided by Randy Southern, Rick Thompson
Designer: Bob Fuller
Cover illustrator: Bob Fuller
Inside illustrator: Paula Becker
Printed in U.S.A.
ISBN: 0-7814-4992-8

CONTENTS

ABOUT THE AUTHORS

Paul Borthwick is minister of missions at Grace Chapel in Lexington, Massachusetts. A former youth pastor and frequent speaker to youth workers, he is the author of several books, including *Organizing Your Youth Ministry* and *Feeding Your Forgotten Soul: Spiritual Growth for Youth Workers* (Zondervan).

Karen Dockrey is a longtime youth worker as well as a prolific author of programs for youth groups, including the *Snap Sessions* series (David C. Cook). Her many books include *Friends: Finding and Keeping Them* (Broadman Press). She lives with her family in Hendersonville, Tennessee.

Steve Hickey served for several years as the junior high minister at Hillcrest Covenant Church in Kansas City. He is studying at North Park Theological Seminary in Chicago.

Mark Oestreicher is the junior high pastor at Calvary Church in Santa Ana, California. He is also a free-lance writer and seminar leader.

Sue Reck is an editor for Chariot Family Products. As a free-lance curriculum writer, she contributed to the *Junior Highs Only* series (David C. Cook). She has worked with young people in Sunday school classes, youth groups, and camp settings.

Tim Richards, a former junior high director and high school youth pastor, is currently pastor of adult ministries at the Sierra Bible Church in Sonora, California. He is also a free-lance curriculum writer.

Tangible Takeaways

1. Geode Rocks

Jesus confronted the Pharisees saying they were "like whitewashed tombs, which look beautiful on the outside but on the inside are full of dead men's bones and everything unclean" (Matt. 23:27). Elsewhere He stressed that His followers should be inwardly pure, saying "Blessed are the pure in heart . . . " (Matt. 5:8).

So, after a session on inward purity or holiness, send everyone home with a Geode rock. If you live near a major city, you can pick some of these up at a rock shop. They are often sold in souvenir shops.

You might want to buy a few larger rocks and then break off some pieces to hand out. Make sure you hand out pieces that have both the outer and the inner stone.

While kids are holding the pieces you gave them, wrap up the session by saying something like this: **These rocks appear to be dark, rough, and even ugly on the outside. Yet what makes them beautiful is the white, blue, and purple crystals on the inside. Take these rocks home. Every time you see them, remember the high value Jesus placed on inward purity. Though you may not feel as if you look great on the outside, what is most important to Jesus is whether or not you have a pure heart.**

2. Get the Lead Out

When you've finished a lesson on gossip, or building others up rather than cutting them down, give each member of your group a pencil. Try to find pencils that have fun designs on them or are fun colors, rather than the basic yellow, number-two type.

Then hand out pieces of paper, and challenge kids to write down as many people as they can think of who they could encourage with their pencils this week. They can also brainstorm different ways to use the pencil (writing someone an encouraging note, drawing a picture for someone, etc.).

Challenge the group to think about the power words and actions can have—positive as well as negative—and encourage them to use their words—and pencils—to build up rather than tear down.

Variation: Also bring in a pencil sharpener (the electric kind will work best). Give kids unsharpened pencils. While they are sharpening them, remind them that it's better to use a sharp pencil (or pen) than a sharp tongue!

3. Fruit Loot

In John, chapter fifteen, Jesus uses the analogy of the vine and its branches (also Matt. 7:15-23). Those branches (Christians) that the gardener (the Father) wants to bear more fruit are pruned. Those that aren't bearing fruit are cut off and thrown into the fire. It is to the Father's glory that we bear much fruit, but we can't do this unless we remain attached to the vine (Jesus).

Prepare several delicious kinds of fruit and set them out on a table before the session begins (get a wide assortment: cantaloupe, grapes, bananas, pineapple, apples, strawberries, kiwi, watermelon, etc.). Don't let anyone eat from the table until after the session. You might need to refrigerate the fruit after showing it off.

After the session, let kids have a feast and then send them home with a banana to eat later. (Some may choose to stick the little round banana sticker (Chiquita, Dole, etc.) on the inside of their Bibles to remind them that they should bear fruit as Christian disciples.

4. Don't Leaf Me Alone

Here's another idea that could be used when studying John 15. Following a study of the vine and the branches (John 15:1-17), display a long plastic (or cloth) vine. If possible, find one with artificial flowers or leaves in a department store or floral shop. Let the vine be long enough to include at least one branch (or leaf) for each youth present.

Ask: **According to John 15:1-17, what does the vine represent? What do the branches represent?** (Look at the leaves if your vine doesn't have obvious branches.)

Which part of the vine are you?

How does Jesus treat His branches?

Have each teen take hold of a leaf or branch on the vine.

Ask: **What does "remain" or "abide" mean in verses 4-10?**

What do you like most about God's love?

What are the advantages of abiding in the vine (vss. 5-17)?

With what specific actions, attitudes, and words do you abide in Jesus, the vine?

Encourage kids to name a different action, attitude, or sentence. As they do, give them each a leaf clipped from the vine to represent a branch. Suggest they mark John 15 in their Bibles with their leaves or keep the leaves in their wallets as a reminder to abide in Jesus throughout their lives.

5. Highlights

After a lesson on studying God's Word, pass out bright highlighter markers. You can buy inexpensive ones at any office supply store.

Encourage kids to highlight verses that really means something to them. Psalm 119 would be a good place to start if kids need ideas. Almost every verse in that chapter makes the point of knowing God's Word and living by it.

After a few minutes, ask students to share the verse they highlighted and why. Encourage them to take the highlighters home and, each day this week, highlight one verse that they would like to think about during the day.

You might direct them to the Book of Proverbs where they will find lots of practical bits of wisdom.

6. Custom Credit Cards

Next time you want to send an idea home with kids, try this idea: Condense the key thought, principle, verse, or commitment to fit on a card the size of a credit card. Write it neatly or, better yet, find a computer with a good printer and have it printed out. You could also include an appropriate illustration from a clip-art book. (If you have access to a copier that reduces and enlarges images, you can make almost any picture fit.)

Make enough copies for everyone in the class. Use a bright, heavy paper for added effect. Have the finished cards laminated (see office supply stores, commercial copy stores, or local schools that laminate their student I. D. cards). The laminated cards will be durable reminders to your kids of the lesson. They can carry them in their wallets, purses, or bookbags.

Here's one example. If your lesson was on Romans 4, you could print Romans 4:24b on one side: "God will credit righteousness—for us who believe in him who raised Jesus our Lord from the dead."

On the other side you could list Scripture verses that might come in handy for kids to use when explaining the plan of salvation to a friend.

7. Magnetic Pulls

During a study of Romans 8:38, 39 display magnets of various strengths. Encourage kids to separate or try to separate each pair.

Ask: **What can separate these magnets?**

When is your relationship with God like (or unlike) each of these pairs?

How do events impact how close we feel to God?

How much do our actions impact how close we feel to God?

Emphasize that no force, event, or action can separate us from God's love, no matter how close or distant we feel. Unlike the

magnets that can be separated, God won't ever pull away from us. However, there might be times when we pull away from Him.

Emphasize that God's love for us is not dependent on our actions or feelings. His love is constant and He will always be there for us.

Call on a volunteer to read Romans 8:38, 39.

Ask: **Which of these crises would most threaten you?**

How does God keep on loving you in the midst of them?

How, besides feelings, do people know God is with them?

Give everyone two magnets of such strength that they are nearly impossible to separate. Check hardware stores or department stores for inexpensive disc magnets. Encourage kids to put these on their locker walls as reminders of the tight bond God has with each of them.

Variation: You may want to intentionally choose a weak magnet as a reminder that God's love is stronger than any physical bond.

8. Yucky Chocolate

Break several bars of unsweetened baking chocolate (available in the baking aisles of grocery stores) into bite-sized pieces and put them on a plate. At the close of a study on temptation or betraying God, pass around the plate of chocolate pieces, identifying it only as "chocolate."

As kids eat the chocolate and react to its bitterness, ask: **What's wrong with this chocolate?**

Why did some of you who got the chocolate plate last, hesitate to eat your piece?

How are your experiences with this chocolate like temptation?

Do you have to taste temptation to understand its dangers?

What makes temptation look so good if it tastes so bad?

How does watching others help you resist the dangers of disobeying God? When does it not help?

Point out that baking chocolate does not contain sugar. Even though it may look and smell good, it leaves a bitter taste that stays a long time. Suggest that temptation is like this—it looks great but there's a lot missing. And it leaves a bitter taste in our "mouths." Once we've eaten it we can't un-eat it. Sometimes we endure long-term bitter experiences as a result of giving in to a single temptation.

Study Proverbs 23:23-35 to illustrate the value of truth over any counterfeit offer of fun.

Have kids discuss ways to discover and live God's truth, including watching what happens when other people choose paths that look good but lead to destruction.

Cut up the box that the chocolate came in and give pieces to kids as reminders to look beyond appearances to the true nature of a person or activity.

Variation: Don't leave kids with a bitter taste in their mouths. Pass around some sweet chocolate. Compare it to the sweetness of God's Word (see Ps. 19:10 or 119:103).

9. Do The Ring Thing

To close a study on God's eternal power or never-ending strength, distribute inexpensive rings, available in toy or party stores. Point out that no matter where you start on the ring, you can keep going around it without end.

Ask: **How is this like God's power?**

How have you seen His power in your life?

Describe the security God gives you.

Scriptures and adaptations that work with rings include:

• Isaiah 40:28-31—Show kids how to make the rings from beads and elastic thread. The right match of bead size and thread makes it possible to thread the elastic without needles. Make sure you try stringing one first, to avoid a mid-meeting flop.

As you distribute materials, challenge kids to search Isaiah 40:31 for three ways God gives us power: power to soar, power to run, power to walk.

Ask: **In what circumstances would you need each?**

How is each equally valuable?

How have you seen each in your experience?

Have kids choose a color for each of these God-given powers and string the rest of the ring in a fourth color that complements the three beads. Suggest that kids wear the rings as reminders that God will equip them to both manage and triumph in everything that happens.

• John 14:18—Emphasize the power of God's presence. Invite brief testimonies on how God's presence has affected your group members. Have volunteers read the verse in a variety of Bible translations.

Ask: **Which phrasing means the most to you right now and why? How do they essentially say the same thing?**

Distribute rings and narrow strips of paper. Encourage kids to write the words of John 14:18 on the paper and use the paper to make a "stone" for the ring. When the stone tears or gets wet, kids can still wear the ring as a reminder of God's care.

10. Heads or Tails?

Have fun flipping coins at the end of a session on commitment or loyalty to God.

Have a volunteer read Deuteronomy 30:19, 20 or Joshua 24:15.

Ask: **How is a choice for God more than luck? More than chance? More than something you do impulsively or spontaneously?**

Why is it a series of decisions?

With what deliberate actions do you show your dedication to God?

Using verses such as Deuteronomy 30:11-20 and Joshua 24:14-27 ask:

What might block a commitment to God?

What might block living out that commitment?

How will you move past obstacles to living out your faith?

Have kids toss their coins in the air and name a way to live their loyalty—before they catch the coin. Repeat with different life areas such as home, school, friendship, work, church.

Encourage kids to keep the coins as a reminder to deliberately choose to follow God. Suggest that every time they see a coin this week, they should think of a specific way God wants them to obey Him that day.

Variation: Start out by playing a game. Give each kid a coin. Have them pair up and flip their coins. If both coins end up with the same side up, the pair of kids can remain in the game; otherwise they are out. Play additional rounds. Award a prize to those who stay in the game the longest. After the game, talk about the difference between deliberately serving God and leaving things up to chance.

11. The Key Thing

This idea is both a challenge and a tangible takeaway.

Near the end of a study on seeking God's guidance, give each group member a key. This key can be duplicated from a meaningful original such as the key to your youth meeting place. It can be a generic key for a diary or suitcase. Or it can be a key that no longer opens an actual lock. Use the key with passages such as Matthew 6:31-34 or Romans 12:1, 2.

If you use the Matthew passage, ask:

According to Matthew 6:33, what is the key to getting what we need in life? (One possibility is to let God lead us and show us how to live.)

What are some of these needs according to 6:31-34? (Food, drink, clothing, good tomorrows.)

What else would you add to this list? (Friends, family, purpose in life, understanding, wisdom.)

How does working toward God's kingdom and walking His path of right living help these happen?

If you use the Romans passage, ask:

How can God tell if someone has offered himself or herself to Him?

Has God changed you? If so, how?

With what actions and attitudes do you think God wants you to offer yourself to Him?

As you discuss the above questions ask:

If putting God first is the key, what are some of the things this key might open in your life? Let kids offer some suggestions.

Then ask:

What color do you associate with putting God first?

One group member may say, "Putting God first is white because He sheds light on every event in my life." Another may say, "Putting God first is red because it takes a heart for obedience." Still another member might say, "Giving oneself to God is green because it's a warm and secure status." Affirm the wisdom of all insights.

Then distribute paint pens and have kids paint their keys with the color(s) they feel best describes putting God first.

Encourage kids to put the keys on their key rings to help them remember that God is willing to guide their actions, attitudes, and decisions.

12. Don't Forget

Use this at the close of a meeting that has focused on helping hurting people. It can be built around a study of Romans 12:15b ("mourn with those who mourn") or Hebrews 13:3 ("Remember those in prison as if you were their fellow prisoners, and those who are mistreated as if you yourselves were suffering").

At the close of the meeting, give each student a picture or some other reminder of people you have considered, those who are much less fortunate than you are. This could be a picture of a famine victim, people injured in an ongoing war, or a homeless person from a city.

Encourage students to carry these pictures with them as reminders of the pain that many other people experience. Tell them that remembering the hurts of others helps us not to complain when we think we have it tough. They should also use them as reminders to pray for hurting people.

Get pictures from sources such as today's newspaper or magazines such as *Time, Newsweek,* or *Life.* Have kids write "Don't Forget!" across the bottoms of their pictures. If possible, have kids mount the pictures or put them in picture frames. This way, they might keep the pictures longer.

Variation: Give each kid a small plastic bag full of rice. Tell kids that this is more food than some people eat in an entire day. Challenge kids to cook and eat this rice sometime during the next week. They shouldn't eat anything else during that meal. As their stomachs growl before their next meal, encourage them to think of those who are hungry all the time.

13. A Phrase for the Journey

Develop short phrases to remind kids about the session topic.

When studying Matthew 5:3 about the blessedness of being spiritually poor, read the New English Bible's "How happy are those who know their need of God." Then give students a phrase for the journey (the rest of the week) that they can recall when they have feelings of inadequacy or fear: "Jesus, I desperately need You" or "Help me, Jesus."

Another example comes from Ephesians 5:18, the command to be constantly filled with the Holy Spirit. Instruct students to bring the phrase into the week—"Jesus, fill me now with Your Holy Spirit"— a prayer that they can pray at anytime—whether before a big test, when they feel angry, or in the face of temptation.

The phrase could be right out of the Bible, like the prayer of the blind men in Matthew 20:30: "Lord, Son of David, have mercy on us!" Or it could be an application of the Scripture truth being taught, such as "Pray Today" from Philippians 4:6, 7 or "Death to selfishness" from Galatians 2:20.

The bullet-like commands from I Thessalonians 5:16-18 ("Be joyful always; pray continually; give thanks in all circumstances") could be combined with I Peter 5:7 ("Cast all your anxiety on him because he cares for you") to yield "Don't worry; be happy" from a biblical point of view.

These phrases could be written on the back of old business cards, or on Post-it notes. Challenge kids to display them until they have the phrases memorized.

14. Polaroid Prayer Cards

In response to biblical examples in which believers supported each other in prayer (Acts 4:23-31), give students a take-away that urges the same in your group.

Take Polaroid pictures of each person; then distribute them so that everyone takes home someone else's picture. Kids should pray throughout the week or month for the people whose pictures they have.

This exercise can work with a study on the fellowship in the body of Christ as seen in Colossians 4 or Ephesians 4. You might also include a meditation on II Corinthians 1:10, 11, in which Paul reminds the Corinthians of his hardships, but speaks confidently of God's deliverance through their prayers. Explain that Christians can better endure hardship when others are praying.

Give each kid time to get prayer requests from the person whose picture he or she has. Kids can write these requests on the back of the photos to refer to at home.

Make sure each kid has time at the beginning of the next session to talk with the person he or she prayed for and to find out if his or her prayers were answered.

15. Mercy In Action Contract

In response to teaching about biblical compassion (Matt. 9:36-38), develop "Mercy in Action" contracts, which kids and leaders will complete at the conclusion of the meeting.

The contracts are a commitment to do some specific act of mercy or compassion. You can include some of these areas in the contract:

• Vision—changing the way I look at or respond to some person

• Finance—making a commitment to help someone out in financial need

• Time—going out of my way to express care for someone in need or an activity such as serving a meal at a shelter for the homeless

The best arrangement is to have students fill out the "contracts" in duplicate, sign both, and keep one for themselves while giving the other to a leader who will hold them accountable to act. The "contracts" can be printed on 5" x 8" card stock to make them more difficult to lose.

▼▼▼▼▼▼▼▼▼▼▼

MERCY IN ACTION CONTRACT

I,

_____
(name)

promise that I will

_____
(describe act of mercy)

for

_____
(name of person)

by

_____
(date)

Signed

_____
(your name)

Signature of witness or partner

_____
(name)

▲ ▲ ▲ ▲ ▲ ▲ ▲ ▲ ▲ ▲ ▲ ▲

These contracts are most effective when kids have a partner to whom they are accountable. Partners should check in with each other in the future.

The contract should look something like the one on page 15. You can copy it if you want.

16. Global Experiences at Home

You can use this idea to follow up a session on the diversity of the body of Christ or on world evangelism (Acts 1:8; Matt. 28:18-20).

Place kids in groups of three to five. Write the names of several international restaurants from your area on separate pieces of paper. Or get menus from these restaurants and give one to each group.

Tell group members and adult leaders that their assignment is to visit or eat a meal at this restaurant before the next meeting. The intent of the visit will be to interact with the owners (to learn about their culture) and/or to try food from another culture.

Or ask several international restaurants to donate food samples for use during this session. This is a great way to dispel cultural stereotypes. If someone says "I don't like Mexican food; it's too spicy and hot"—give that person a plate filled with bland refried beans!

Or instead of having kids eat ethnic food, have them sign up to go to worship services next week at some ethnic churches in the area. Worshiping together with Christians of other cultures is a great way to teach about the great multicultural worship service of Revelation 7:9.

17. Mirror, Mirror

After a session on self-esteem or self-image, have kids paint personal messages about God's love for them onto small mirrors that you provide. Supply lots of thin brushes and colorful paints (that will stick to the mirror; test it). Kids might paint "God loves me just the way I am" or similar messages on their mirrors. Encourage kids to come up with unique messages. Have kids display their handiwork and describe one thing about themselves that is unique.

Encourage kids to remember this message every time they look in the mirror: God created you exactly as you are for a reason and He loves you as you are.

18. Plastic Lizards

After a session on consistency in the Christian life, hand out small plastic toy lizards. Tell kids to imagine that the creatures are chameleons (if they're not). Explain that a chameleon actually changes its skin color depending on its environment. For example, if a chameleon lives in a grassy area, it will turn greenish; in a rocky place, it turns brownish. The chameleon adapts to its environment so that it is not easily spotted. It blends in with everything else.

Ask: **How are Christians sometimes like chameleons?**

Christians who are afraid of being rejected or ridiculed sometimes try to blend in with non-Christians. They "change colors" to suit the situation. At church, they might appear red hot for the Lord, while at school or work they appear green—like non-Christians.

Let the toy lizard remind your kids that God doesn't want us to be chameleon-like in our loyalty to Him (Revelation 3:15). In the Christian life there is no middle ground; you are either for God or against Him.

Variation: Before the session, buy a live chameleon from a local pet store. Bring it to show to your group. Talk about the positive and negative ways that Christians can act like chameleons. The negative way is described above; a positive way is described in I Corinthians 9:19-23, where Paul talks about becoming all things to all people in order to bring them salvation.

19. Key Chains

After a session on grace or salvation, give each kid in your group a key chain. Take a minute or two and have the kids name as many things as they can think of that have keys (a house, a car, a padlock, etc.). Then reemphasize that the key to salvation is what Christ did for us on the cross. We can't get to heaven by our own good works, good looks, or good luck.

Remind kids as they leave that the key to salvation is God's grace and love. Encourage them to remember this each time they use a key on their key chains.

20. To Top It All Off

Set up a table with all types of supplies—clothes paint, glue, glitter, markers, buttons, etc. Give each kid a plain white painter's cap. Explain that kids can decorate their hats any way they want to, except it must be done in a way that symbolizes one of their unique talents or gifts.

When they've completed their hats, ask volunteers to display their hats and to explain why they decorated it the way they did.

Wrap up by reading Ephesians 4:7-13. Emphasize that each of us has been given a special gift, and no one gift is any more important than, or can survive without, the others.

21. Blank Tapes

After a talk on the influence of the media, give each member of your group a blank cassette tape.

Ask: **What happens when you record something on the tape and then play it back?** (You hear exactly what you recorded.)

Remind kids that our minds are like those blank tapes. What we take in is recorded and eventually comes back out.

Read Philippians 4:8, 9 and ask kids why they think God would want us to fill our minds with things that are true, noble, right, etc.

Challenge kids to really think about what they're going to record onto their new blank cassette tapes—and their minds—and to record things that are true, noble, right, pure, lovely, admirable, excellent, and praiseworthy.

22. Crucifixion Challenge

Walking through the events leading up to, and including, the crucifixion of Jesus Christ can be a powerful experience for teens. Explain in detail everything Jesus went through. Most students, even those raised in a church, have not fully understood what Jesus went through for them.

Talk about the emotional pain of having Jesus' friends deny knowing Him and the pain of having the guards ridicule Him. Explain the process of being whipped with a cat-o'-nine-tails, and the significance of thirty-nine lashes. If you don't know this information yourself, look in a Bible dictionary or encyclopedia.

When you get to the description of being nailed onto the cross, give a nail to each student. Try to find large ones at the hardware store (probably about six inches long and 1/4 inch in diameter). Have students lightly press the tip of the nail against their wrists and imagine what it would be like to have these pounded in with no anesthetic. Be sure you explain the process of death by crucifixion (suffocation).

Let kids take their nails home to remind them of Jesus' great love for them.

23. Baptism Capsules

This is a great opener that gives kids something to take home. The trick is finding the capsules.

Go to a toy store and look for small capsules that, when dropped in water, expand into small, colored, foam objects. They usually come in groupings such as: sports, wild animals, sea creatures, boats and ships, etc. Every package should also have several colors. You'll want to purchase enough for every student to have one capsule. You'll also want to get as many different categories or groupings as possible.

Give one capsule to each person; have kids find people with capsules of the same color.

Once kids are in small groups, have them hold up their capsules while you explain what your church believes about baptism.

Before you have kids "immerse" their capsules into bowls of water you have provided, have them try to guess what they think the capsules will turn into.

Once the foam shapes expand, say: **When we're baptized, we identify with Christ, and our spiritual life grows.**

Now have kids get into groups according to the category of the foam object (cite the categories if necessary). Then explain: **Identifying with Christ puts you with like-minded Christians who support one another.**

Let teens take home their foam pieces to remember the significance of baptism.

24. Sucker Talk

Study the life of Demas, who was a "sucker for the world."

We don't know very much about Demas. In Philemon 24 he is mentioned by Paul as one of Paul's disciples. Paul mentions him once again in Colossians 4:14. After establishing Demas' relationship with Paul, have students think about what it would be like to spend a year or two with Paul. Ask them what effect it might have on their spiritual lives.

Then read II Timothy 4:9, 10. This is where we find out that Demas deserted Paul because of his love for the world. Tell your teens that Demas was a sucker. Ask them to speculate what might have drawn Demas away.

Then pass out suckers as a reminder to the students. They'll probably all eat them as they leave. But that's okay; it will at least take the lesson a few steps beyond your classroom!

25. Soil Testing

Talk to your students about spiritual self-examination using the parable of the soil in Luke 8:4-8.

Take a bean and throw it against the wall in your room. Then ask your students to speculate on how well the bean will grow. When they've finished, ask:

So, what is wrong with that bean, that it won't grow?

The obvious answer is that there is nothing wrong with the bean, only the way it was planted, or the "soil" it encountered. Explain that the same is true with God's Word—the Bible. There's nothing wrong with the Bible, but its effect on our lives depends greatly upon the "soil" it falls on.

Study the different types of soil, and have kids make comparisons to types of people. Then give a bean to each person. Ask:

What type of soil are you?

Instruct kids to put the beans in their pockets or purses to remind them of your lesson.

Variation: Stage a contest to see whose bean can grow into the tallest plant in one, two, or three months. To do this, kids will need to plant the seeds in a paper cup and keep them on a windowsill. When kids report back, ask those with the largest plants to talk about the secret of their success. Draw some parallels to the Christian life.

26. The Scars of Sin

Try this to drive home the point when talking about the consequences of sin.

Have a small flat piece of wood ready for each student. Bring enough spray-on (quick drying) wood stain to cover each piece.

During the session, give everyone a piece of wood. Spread out some newspaper on the floor and allow each teen to spray his or her piece of wood. While the stain is drying, talk about the effects of sin.

After you're done, open a box of nails (you'll also need to have a few hammers). Explain that kids should symbolize sin by pounding nails into their nicely finished pieces of wood. Your students should enjoy this. Have each one pound three or four nails. Make sure they don't pound them through to the floor of your room unless you're looking for an opportunity to be excused from your teaching responsibilities. The nails only need to be pounded in about a quarter of an inch.

Than talk briefly about the forgiveness of sin that Christ offers us. Instruct teens to symbolize this by removing the nails from the wood (use claw hammers for this). Removing the nails should be fairly simple if they haven't been pounded in too far.

After all the nails have been pulled out, point out that the board isn't as nice as when you started. Explain that while our sins are gone and completely forgiven, there may still be scars (consequences).

Have your students take their pieces of wood home and put them in a prominent place where they will be reminded regularly about the need to avoid sin in order to avoid the consequences of sin.

One final note: If your class is extremely large, or if you just don't have the time to prepare all the pieces of wood, this idea can be accomplished more easily by using one large piece of wood.

Spray and dry the wood before your session begins. Have each student (or a few volunteers) pound nails and remove them. Then give everyone a nail to take home.

27. Hair Today, Home Tomorrow

Give everyone in the group a plastic comb. (These can be purchased very inexpensively at most grocery or discount stores.)

Then set out some small paintbrushes and various colors of paint. Give kids a chance to paint their combs. They can use whatever designs they want; but somewhere on the comb the kids have to write down how many hairs they think they have on their heads.

When everyone is finished, have volunteers display their combs and reveal the numbers they wrote down.

Have fun with this. For instance, if a person guesses that he has 100,000 hairs on his head, you might walk up behind him, pretend to pick a couple of hairs off his shoulder, and say, "You'd better change that to 99,998." Most people have between 50,000 and 75,000, but keep in mind that the average person sheds 68 hairs in 24 hours!

Encourage kids to take the combs home and put them some place where they'll be seen often. The combs will serve as reminders that God cares about us so much that He knows how many hairs are on our heads (Matt. 10:30).

28. Ties That Bind

After a session on racism (or getting along with everyone), distribute multicolored shoelaces. As a symbol of their willingness to accept people of all colors, have group members replace their current shoelaces with the multicolored ones. Or kids can tie them around their wrists if they aren't wearing shoes that need laces.

Emphasize that the shoelaces should be more than just a symbol; they should be a reminder to demonstrate acceptance. As a group, list ways kids can demonstrate acceptance of people of other races. The list might include things like eating lunch with someone of another race, stopping someone from telling a racial joke, starting conversations with people of other races, etc.

Group
Affirmations

1. Make-believe City

As students move toward their senior year in high school, many feel anxious because they are facing major decisions about college and careers. You have the opportunity to make your youth group a place for kids to develop dreams and test their gifts and talents and to reduce their anxiety. Use this affirming activity to help your kids take a good look at each other and a good look toward the future.

Pair kids up with someone they know fairly well. Give them five minutes to decide what role each will play in the make-believe city that you are creating. They must not only pick roles but also list at least three reasons for their decision. Here are a few examples:

• Ted will become a scientist because:
(1) he has a great eye for detail (he can pick a hair out of a hamburger from ten feet away);
(2) he has an interest in biology; and
(3) he gets goods grades.

• Mary will become a youth pastor because:
(1) she is very energetic and outgoing;
(2) she brings more friends that anyone else to youth group; and
(3) she is able to explain some of the more difficult parts of the Bible to those of us who don't understand.

After all kids have picked a role for their partners, have them sit in a circle and take turns introducing their partners. Other students can add extra reasons or stories as to why this would be a good choice. Everyone should leave feeling affirmed, valuable, and possibly more aware of gifts that others can see but they haven't yet noticed.

Keep a master list of all the different roles (jobs) that people will hold in your make-believe city. Discuss what other types of people are needed to make the city fully functional. Challenge kids to invite those kinds of people to church.

2. Group Mural

If there is a wall in the youth room that can use a good painting, or even if there is a free wall to hang big sheets of paper, this activity is perfect.

Devote a whole session to creating a group mural. Call everyone ahead of time so that as many people as possible can come. When they arrive, begin by saying that they are going to create a mural that should tell people one hundred years from now as much about your group as possible. Ask them to paint images that provide information about the group, and individuals in the group. Tell them it's important to give an accurate rendering of your youth group so that people who live a century from now have a better understanding of who you are.

Kids can paint figures of themselves or other images, but they must portray the personalities and qualities of those in the group as well as the uniqueness of the group as a whole. Let the mural dry and leave it up for awhile (probably not a century), so kids can admire the details and their place in the history of the group.

3. Special Feature

Often the evening news or the newspaper will spotlight a certain person, place, or event. These features are interesting and different. Even local newspapers may focus on high school students who are exceptional athletes or musicians.

Here are a couple of ways to run "special features" on the kids in your group who might never make it into their local newspaper.

If possible, start a regular column in your church newsletter highlighting a different student or two each month. Include things such as:

- an interview with their best friends
- a family summary
- pet stories
- accomplishments
- interests
- best book read or movie seen
- favorite verses
- funniest thing that ever happened to him or her
- sports abilities

Also include a word from you and a fun picture of them involved at church. This gives the rest of the church a chance to meet the teenagers and gives certain kids a much-needed avenue for positive attention.

The parents of the featured student will surely cherish this piece in a scrapbook for years to come. This could also be done on a bulletin board in the church hallway and could include many pictures from the students' lives.

4. Newspaper Ad

For the cost of a birthday card, you can give your kids a really special treat—their own newspaper ads.

A week before a person's birthday, pass around a sheet of paper to the other members of the group. Have each person write one word that describes a quality he or she appreciates about that individual.

Then, depending on how many contributions you have, or how much you want to spend, include the whole list or a few of the best descriptions as part of a personal ad in your local newspaper. An ad might read like this:

Angela, you're bright, funny, caring.
Happy Birthday from First Church Youth.

Bill, you're honest, helpful, friendly.
Happy B-day from your friends at church.

5. Bulletin Board

You can help new kids get to know your group more quickly and provide a fun way to highlight their traits, talents, and achievements with a picture bulletin board. What makes this display special though isn't the pictures; it's the captions.

Take individual pictures of all the kids. Let them ham this up all they want. Next, pick a caption sentence to be completed. For instance:

"The funniest thing I ever saw (name) do was . . . "
"The best thing about (name) is . . . "
"(Name) really enjoys . . . "

Pass a piece of paper around for each person with his or her name written clearly at the bottom. As it goes around the circle, each person writes a thought or comment at the top of the page, then folds it down and passes it to the next person.

When finished, collect all the sheets. If your group is large, break them into several smaller groups and divide the names among them.

During the week, pick one or two of the best for each individual and write it on a slip of paper under his or her picture. At your next meeting kids will enjoy looking for their pictures to see what was written.

A variation of this idea would be to let kids fill out a slip about themselves stating an achievement they are proud of or why they like the youth group. You might want to periodically give kids a new topic to respond to and change the captions. Whenever you change the captions, shuffle the pictures so kids have to keep looking to find themselves and others. This will help them see people they might not normally pay attention to.

One caution: Don't let the board be abused. If somebody's picture gets a mustache drawn on it or rude comment written under it, put up a new picture immediately (you might even want to get double prints when you first have your film processed so you're prepared). Remember, this board is to encourage kids; not embarrass them.

6. People Poster

Each week, create a huge poster that spotlights one of your teens. Use colorful markers to add interesting facts about the person-of-the-week.

Interview both the person and a friend of this person ahead of time to discover what to write on the poster. Consider clearing what you plan to write with the person ahead of time to keep from embarrassing or exposing private information.

These sample questions move from simple to deep with the assumption that your kids will become more comfortable as they talk:

FOR THE TEEN IN THE SPOTLIGHT:
1. What school do you attend?
2. What is your favorite subject in school? Least favorite?
3. What do you most like to do?
4. Why are you glad to be a Christian?
5. What do you like about being a part of this group?
6. What do you like about yourself or your life?
7. Do you have photographs or mementoes to add to your people poster?

FOR THE FRIEND:
1. What do you like best about ___?
2. What good things do people say about ___ at school?
3. What do you especially like doing with ___?
4. How does ___ express faith in Jesus Christ?

5. Why are people glad to have ___ as part of our group?
6. What is your favorite memory of or with ___?
7. What else should be on a people poster about ___?

Consider making some interesting people-poster variations such as shaping the poster to look like the person with the height, hair color, and one other distinguishing characteristic of the youth.

Or, shape the poster like a favorite activity of the featured teen.

Or, hang a rectangular poster in the doorway and invite the teen to break the paper to start the meeting. If they prefer not to break their posters, leave one side unattached so they can read and enter as they arrive.

Keep a running list of teens-of-the-week to be sure you leave no one out. Add visitors to the list and call them the week before you plan to spotlight them to encourage them to be present.

If you publish a teen newsletter, repeat the teen-of-the-week information there.

7. Affirmation Games

Use a contemporary game format to increase the comfort and effectiveness of affirmation. Examples include:

• The person being affirmed rolls a letter cube (available in a *Boggle* game, or other word games). Other members of the group write on paper four characteristics they like in the person that begin with the rolled letter. Each member who beats the (one-minute) timer with four authentic compliments, gets a point.

If your group is large, play in teams. If your group is small, accumulate points individually. Then celebrate the "best affirmer" or "most affirming team"—an affirmation in itself.

• Divide kids into two teams. Choose a person on one team to be affirmed. That team lists ten personality characteristics they like about this person. The other team then shouts out what they think the ten things are. If they guess all ten things before two minutes is up, they win points. The affirmed person gets many more than ten compliments and the entire group enjoys the process.

• Each group member writes down at least two compliments for the person being affirmed, each on a separate sheet of paper. Gather and shuffle these compliments. Invite volunteers to come to the front of the group, choose one compliment, and draw it (*Pictionary*-style) for the group to guess. The one who guesses draws the next compliment.

8. Compliments Galore

Change the physical setup of affirmation to increase both giver and receiver comfort. Try these variations on the you-sit-in-the-chair-while-we-tell-you-what-we-like format:

• Divide into teams of two members or more. Choose a person to be affirmed, but let her stay in her team where she can watch her team's process. Teams compete with other teams to write the greatest number of authentic compliments on a single person. Repeat for all present, rotating among teams.

• Give each team ninety seconds to compose at least nine compliments for the one being affirmed. Repeat for each person. While this is happening, the affirmed person should privately write what s/he likes about himself/herself. Give all written compliments to the affirmed person to keep.

• Each team compliments a different area: one team does appearance, another does personality characteristics; another names ways the affirmed person lives out Christian commitment; and so on. Present these in written form to the affirmed.

• Direct pairs of kids to compose limericks about each other. A limerick is a five-line poem. The first two lines and the last line rhyme and are a bit longer than the third and fourth line. The third and fourth line rhyme and are a bit shorter. Here are two examples:

> There once was a person named Randy,
> Who was sweeter than Halloween candy.
> He liked to play sports,
> And always wore shorts,
> And with cars he was really quite handy.
>
> Sue is a very good friend.
> She's always quite willing to lend
> A book or CD;
> Some cash if need be.
> Her friendship is real, not pretend.

9. Paper Possibilities

Use paper in a variety of ways to affirm your teens:

• *Spell out compliments*. Spotlight one teen per meeting. Prior to the meeting, cut the letters of the person's name, using large block letters. Make each letter the size of a full sheet of construction paper, or larger. Challenge the group to fill each letter with compliments about the person beginning with that letter.

• *Celebration cards*. List all the events in life worth celebrating. Possibilities include: getting a driver's license, resisting a temptation, birthdays, finishing middle school or high school, finding the courage to live for Christ in a new way, passing a hard test, getting a good teacher, and more. As a group, or with a committee of interested kids, design postcards or greeting cards for each event. Draw the postcards on the front of a white note card. Draw the greeting cards on white paper with black pen, first folding the paper twice and then writing on the front and inside page.
Before completing the drawings and greetings, open the sheet to be certain everything you've drawn or written appears on one side. Once complete, duplicate on a photocopy machine and fold. Keep the postcards and greeting cards in a central location and show kids where to place the cards for mailing. Challenge them to listen for each other's good events and to send a card when one occurs.

• *Clippings*. Every time teens appear by name or photograph in the newspaper, cut out the article, laminate it, and present it to your teen. Put a reliable young person or team in charge of this process as an affirmation of their ability to find every article and name. If you don't have access to a laminating machine, use clear contact plastic.

• *Birthday greetings*. Mail a bundle of compliments to teens on their birthdays. This can be a single card secretly passed around the week before, or a series of cards created by a group of youth. If you can afford the postage, consider mailing a card a day for the week prior to each birthday.

10. Affirm the Group

Display paper large enough so everyone can draw at the same time. Direct kids to draw, describe or doodle what the group does right. The specifics can depend on the theme you're studying—if unity, let the assignment be "How our group builds unity." If the theme is welcoming new friends, let the assignment be "How our group makes new friends feel welcome" or "a time this group made me feel welcome." If your theme is obedience, let the assignment be, "How this group frees me to be an authentic Christian."

Affirming the whole group at once has several advantages:

• The group feels a sense of oneness and purpose.

• There's no sense of "I got more compliments than you did."

• Youth feel a part of a team effort. Because everyone writes at once, no one feels put on the spot.

• The affirmation gives goals to shoot for and ways to improve.

As with any affirmation activity, insist that comments be sincere and positive.

11. Notes of Encouragement

In keeping with the teachings of Romans 12:10 ("Be devoted to one another in brotherly love") or Romans 12:12c ("faithful in prayer"), give each student seven names of youth group members. Instruct kids to take these names with them for the subsequent week.

Each student is then assigned a job. Their task is to find some way every day to encourage that person specifically. Give students simple examples like an encouraging phone call or a personal note.

For this exercise to work best, tell students that they must make a personal contact with their affirmation target. In other words, breathing a prayer for them is not enough.

In addition, instruct students to be specific in their encouragement. Their goal is to offer an affirmation for some specific act or character trait. "You are a great human being" is not a specific affirmation whereas, "I really appreciated the way that you reached out to that lonely kid in the lunchroom today" is.

Encouragement notes like this work best when you take away as many student excuses as possible. Giving students cards that they can send, providing addresses, phone numbers, and stamps can all contribute to the success of this endeavor. In addition, it is wisest to keep the encouragement on a same-sex basis so as not to provide a platform for undesired or awkward, one-way romances.

12. Parental Appreciation

These activities affirm kids and teach them how to affirm.

At the close of the meeting, give students time and materials to write notes of appreciation, which they can give (or you can send) to their parents. You might want to suggest some things that students can include for which they are thankful—economic support, love, protection, etc. The best notes, however, are designed to say something personal and specific from student to parent.

An alternate way to affirm is through a "parents swap night." At this activity, have parents get in small groups and teens get in small groups. Have them share one thing for which they especially appreciate or are thankful for their teen/parent.

Then combine half the parents from one small group with half the teens from another small group. Do the same with the other small groups. You may have to do some extra shuffling to make sure that parents are not with their own teens. Have these groups discuss again the things that they are thankful for—parents should talk about their teens and teens should talk about their parents.

Then, at the close of the meeting, put the parents together with their own teens. Both parents and teens should repeat what they have said about each other. This is a great way to get family members to express appreciation for each other.

Variation: If you're going on a retreat, contact at least one parent for each kid in your group. Ask those parents to write notes of affirmation to their children. Each note could start with, "Something I really appreciate about you is . . . " or, "I probably don't tell you this enough, but I . . . " Collect these notes and hand them out to the kids at an appropriate time.

13. The Perfect Youth Group Member

This activity illustrates the way Christians can contribute as part of the Body of Christ (I Cor. 12, Rom. 12, I Pet. 4, Eph. 4).

Choose one characteristic or attribute of each group member to affirm, and from this list, create "the composite and complete youth group member." In other words, define how the group is enhanced by the positive individual contribution of each member.

In this exercise, the leader must make sure that every member of the group is included and affirmed. The goal is to help group members identify some quality or gift that they specifically and uniquely contribute to the group. Try to steer clear of superficial things like good looks or athletic prowess.

Instead, build the composite youth group member out of things like ˹rah's ability to show mercy to hurting people, John's wisdom in ˹ng decisions, Kyle's outgoing spirit of hospitality, and Bill's sense of humor. Look for other qualities like a worshipful spirit, perseverance, grace under pressure, or the ability to bring peace in a "storm."

This activity works especially well on retreats or at camps, or in the formation of small group mission teams where every member needs to be affirmed with respect to what he or she offers the group.

14. Secret Admirer

At the close of the meeting, hand out sealed envelopes. Each envelope should contain one group member's name. Kids are to pray for the names they get—without revealing whose names they received. They should pray for these people for one weekend, week, month, or some other designated period of time. They should also find ways to affirm each other.

This idea can work especially well on a weekend retreat or during some period of time where students have a lot of exposure to each other (perhaps a mission trip, summer camp, or during school vacation). Students can write anonymous notes, send little gifts, or look for ways to serve the person without being noticed.

Throughout the time period, have people share how they are being encouraged and affirmed by their secret admirers, and offer some new ideas to students on how they can go out of their way to affirm and serve someone else.

At the close of the affirmation period, have people share together how it felt to be served and loved without knowing who was offering the support. This can be used as a powerful illustration of how God loves us even when we do not respond and when we do not deserve His love.

Then reveal the identity of the secret admirers, who can share with each other what it felt like to serve without reciprocation.

Note: This affirmation exercise should probably be done between same-sex pairings.

15. Affirmation Tally

Tell students at the close of a meeting that they will be working together for a certain time period. A weekend retreat would be an ideal place to introduce this on Friday night, but it could also be used over another designated period—like during the time between now and your next meeting. Their task is affirmation.

Their goal is the implementation of Ephesians 4:29: "Do not let any unwholesome talk come out of your mouths, but only what is helpful for building others up according to their needs, that it may benefit those who listen."

The way that they will implement this verse is through keeping a tally on themselves (or as a small group). Individuals or groups will score their language as follows:

+2 For every word of specific encouragement or affirmation given to someone else.

+1 For every time they speak words of affirmation to a third party about someone else; in other words, positive "gossip."

-1 For any comment of a self-denigrating nature (to teach students not to put themselves down in order to be funny).

-2 For insults or hurtful humor spoken to someone else.

-3 For negative words spoken about some else to a third party (i.e., gossip or slander).

At the conclusion of the tally time, share the scores. Discuss together how negative talk is so much more a part of our culture than positive affirmation. Talk together about how speaking positively about others in an effort to build them up is a Christian discipline and not something that comes naturally.

Pray together as well for the ability to implement Ephesians 4:29 regularly.

16. And the Award Goes To . . .

At the beginning of the year, have your group create an award. Explain that this award will be given out weekly to a person in your group who best lived out or acted on the lesson from the previous week.

The group can come up with a fun name for the award and what they will use for the "trophy." Have a place, on the award itself if possible or on a separate piece of paper, to keep track of who received the award and what he or she did to merit it.

Establish a system for determining who should get the award each week. One way would be to have kids nominate one another and having a group of adults select who actually gets it. You might want to give some other tangible benefit to the award winner, like first in line for treats, not having to read anything out loud, etc.

Some possible award names might be:

• The amazing apple of application award
• The fabulous finger of faith award
• CHOF (Christian Hall of Fame)
• The CIA (Christian in Action) award

17. Brick by Brick

Cover one wall with a huge sheet of paper that looks like a wall made of bricks. At the top of the wall, write: **Encourage one another and build each other up. I Thessalonians 5:11.**

Give the kids a bunch of markers, pens, and pencils, and have them fill in the bricks, starting at the bottom of the wall, by writing in each brick something positive about another member of the group. (Make sure they know these need to be personality traits, not physical traits.)

Leave the wall up over a period of weeks and see how high the group can build each other up.

18. Christmas Cheer

During Christmas, instead of having the traditional "secret pals" or "secret angels" who leave each other gifts, put up a wall or tree of envelopes, one envelope for each person in your group. The kids can put their names on their envelopes and decorate them however they wish before the envelopes are put on the wall (or tree).

During the Christmas season, challenge the kids to leave Christ-centered, encouraging notes for each other in their envelopes. This can help bring your group closer together and help them focus on the true meaning of the season.

19. Compliment Toss

Have everyone sit in a circle. Using a ball, beanbag, or other tossable item, toss each other compliments. Have the person holding the beanbag toss it to someone across the circle, and as he or she does, give that person a compliment. (Again, emphasize that these are to be personality traits, not physical traits.)

The person who caught the compliment then does the same as he or she tosses the bag to someone else. To really keep things moving, have the entire group clapping a beat that the tosses must follow.

As the compliments are flying, be sure to keep an eye open so that each member of the group receives the bag at least once.

20. Surprise Party

To affirm your entire group, throw a surprise party for it. Pick a time of year that is fairly party-less and when kids are typically in the doldrums (the span between Christmas vacation and spring break often gets long for kids).

Let the kids know that the celebration is for no other reason than that you love them and appreciate them and want them to know that they are loved by Christ.

21. Guess Who?

This fun activity will focus your group on "who we are."

Before the session, secretly pull several students into your office area (where the photocopier is) and photocopy their faces. Make sure they don't open their eyes. And make sure they smash their faces right down on the glass—this makes for some pretty hilarious results. You'll also want to keep the participants from seeing any of the copies until later. One final thing—clean smudges off the glass on the copier!

With a bottle of white correction fluid, paint a number on the black space of every photocopy. Make a list of the students and their corresponding numbers as you go (you might not be able to tell who they all are later!).

Now tape the finished products around your room. Pass out blank paper and pencils or pens to each person in your group.

Tell kids to number down the left side of their page (the number of copies you've taped up). Then say:

Maybe you think you know most of the students in our group. Let's see if you can recognize them in these slightly strange portraits.

Let kids mill around the room, writing names next to each number on their page. Then, after most teens seem to be done, regroup and have them reveal the correct answers. Have kids in the photocopies stand when you read their names. Have other kids call out words of affirmation as each person stands.

Variation: If your group is small, photocopy everyone's face. After revealing who's who, have kids write words of affirmation and encouragement on the back of each person's portrait. Send these home with kids as tangible reminders of all their friends in the group.

22. Letter Writing

Many group affirmation activities have a temporary effect. This activity can have a longer-lasting impact. It works best with groups of forty kids or less.

Write each person's name on a slip of paper, fold the papers, and put them in a box or hat. Have each kid draw a name. Make sure no one draws his or her own name.

Hand out blank paper and pencils or pens to each person. Then instruct kids to write a letter of encouragement to the people whose names they drew . They should use these three sentence starters:

1. The thing I appreciate about you is . . .
2. What you add to our group is . . .
3. Remember when . . . (a fun memory)

After the letters are done, collect them and mail them to the appropriate recipients. Make sure no one is left out!

Variation 1: Have kids write similar letters to their parents. This way, the paragraph starters could be:

1. I have the most fun with you when . . .
2. Your best qualities are . . .
3. Thank you for . . .

Again, it's best if you collect the letters and mail them for your students.

Variation 2: In advance, have parents write letters to their kids using the same three statements listed in Variation 1 above. Collect and distribute them at the close of a session on parents.

23. Common Ground

Often, a major road block to unity in a youth group is when students don't think they have anything in common with other teens in the group. This fun exercise forces them to find things in common.

Divide your group into single gender groups of four to six students each. Then pass out one sheet of paper and one pencil to each group.

Down the left side of the paper, have someone in each group write the following categories:

1. Food
2. Game
3. TV show

4. Movie
5. School subject
6. Song
7. Way to spend Saturday
8. Sport
9. Pizza topping
10. Store

Now have them make two columns alongside these categories. Label one "Like" and one "Dislike." Then tell kids that their task is to come up with a "like" and a "dislike" that they can all agree on for each category. If you want to make it a competition, see which group can complete the assignment first.

After all the groups are finished, have them report their common ground.

24. Affirmation Raps

Have kids sit in a circle on the floor. Give each person a few minutes to come up with a brief rap that boasts about the person on his or her right. Rather than boasting about a physical attribute (beauty, having a great body, etc.), each person should concentrate on boasting about the person's personality or about a special memory he or she has of the person.

Each person's rap should be short (no more than four lines). After all the raps have been performed, discuss how it feels to have your good points recognized and remembered by your peers.

If necessary, use the following example to give kids an idea of what you're looking for.

"When you're talking sense of humor
You gotta mention Joe's;
He made me laugh so hard
That milk shot out my nose!"

25. When You're Too Cheap to Send the Very Best

If you have a lot of kids in your group, buying birthday cards for all of them can get expensive. So, for the sake of economy (and fun), you might want to consider creating a "traveling birthday card." All you need is a very large piece of poster board and markers of several colors.

On somebody's birthday, pass the card and one marker around, letting group members write or draw their birthday wishes on the card. Then at the end of the session, present the card to the birthday person and let him or her take it home for the week. For the next person's birthday, use the same card and a marker of a different color. (You may even want to let each group member pick the color he or she wants for his or her birthday.)

Continue until the card is *completely* full. Your kids will probably enjoy the challenge of squeezing as much use out of the card as possible.

Challenges and Devotions

1. A Dollar for Your Thoughts

For many teenagers, their self worth is closely tied into their financial ability to buy the right clothes. That is why some teens welcome the news that in God's eyes they are acceptable no matter what *things* they have.

Realistically though, five minutes after they hear this good news, they forget it when someone they are trying to impress walks by.

Here is a simple way to encourage them to think differently about money. Print up eye-catching wallet (or purse) inserts. These are little green sheets of paper, the size and shape of a dollar bill, which creatively and clearly say: **A person's worth does not depend his or her possessions.** (You may even want to print Luke 12:15 on this insert.)

Whenever kids open their purses or wallets, the insert will remind them that what they do or don't own has no effect on God's love for them. It may even save them a few bucks now and then.

Challenge kids to keep these reminders in their purses/wallets for at least a month and to keep a running tally of how many dollars they spend on themselves versus others.

2. Pain, Pain Go Away

Distribute paper and pens. Have kids draw or describe the pain of someone they know who is hurting (it may be themselves). Assure kids that they can keep their writings or drawings as private as they want to keep them.

Ask: **What kind of pain did you write or draw?**

Tell kids to tear their papers in four or five pieces as they describe the pain written or drawn there. If no one wants to share, you could suggest some of the following and have kids rip their papers up silently:

- My grandmother died and I miss her.
- My teacher yelled at me and I feel dumb.
- I feel ugly and worry that people don't like me.
- I'm lonely and don't know how to stop the lonely feelings.
- Since the accident my legs hurt almost all the time.
- I have so much to do that I fear I'll never finish.

Display tape and ask: **Can we make any difference in people's pain? How specifically can we help heal a friend's pain? How might we prevent pain in the first place? How is receiving a friend's help like receiving God's help?**

Call on a volunteer to read Galatians 5:13-15 and 6:1, 2, while the others follow along in their Bibles and underline helping actions.

Invite volunteers to display the pieces of their pain picture/description. If they want to keep the specifics of the pain private, suggest they display the pieces backside up. Direct selected members of the group to repair the pain picture with tape. To place tape on the pain picture, they must name a specific way to heal that pain. Point out passages like Romans 12 and Colossians 3 for ideas.

When the "pain" has all been taped back together, ask:

How does knowing or not knowing the details of the pain impact how we help?

Can we help even when we don't totally understand? (Yes, through listening, encouraging, caring, etc.)

Point out the scars that remain on the pictures. Ask:

Why is preventing pain better than healing it?

How can we prevent pain?

What can we do to more healthily move through pain we can't prevent?

Write these preventers on fresh clean pieces of paper. Challenge youth to see themselves as pain preventers and pain healers.

Direct them to choose an action they'll do to be a pain preventer (see Gal. 5:15) and an action they will take to be a pain healer. Suggest they write these on the backs of their mended papers. Ask kids to tell or show you their two actions as they leave the room.

3. You Need Fleesl

Ask kids:

What do you think would help a Christian most if he/she really wanted to beat temptation? Kids will probably suggest things like prayer, reading their Bible, and getting help from friends.

After a brief discussion tell them: **One of the best ways to beat temptation is so simple that even your dogs understands it. It's** *fleas.* You might want to stop for a moment while this truth sinks in and thoughtfully reach over to pick something out of the kid's hair next to you (make sure it's a kid who can take the joke).

The Bible actually has quite a bit to say about fleas. Let's look at a few verses. Have the verses written out ahead of time on 3 x 5 cards so you can pass them to volunteers to read aloud for the group. With the first verse kids will realize the wordplay between "flea" and "flee."

- II Timothy 2:22 (flee youthful lusts)
- I Corinthians 6:18 (flee sexual immorality)

- I Corinthians 10:14 (flee idolatry)
- I Timothy 6:9-11 (flee greed)

Take time after each verse is read to discuss what specific things kids are to flee from. Make sure they are able to relate this to their daily lives.

Also, discuss how a person could "flee" in specific situations. It may mean getting out of a car if the driver wants to do something you know isn't right. It may mean agreeing not to be alone with your boyfriend or girlfriend in private place where you might be tempted to sin.

Close by making the point that often the most courageous thing a Christian can do when faced with temptation is RUN! This isn't cowardly or immature. The apostle Paul who penned all the verses they just read was one of the boldest and most godly men of his day. He willingly went to Rome to face execution for the sake of Christ. But persecution and temptation are two different things. When our faith in Jesus is laughed at, we should stand. When our minds or bodies are being tempted, we should run. Being a strong Christian means having a healthy case of "flees."

4. Reach Out and Touch a Missionary

This idea requires some up front preparation time, but will create a unique opportunity to discuss prayer and missions.

Lots of newer telephones come with a speaker that allows a group to listen in on a conversation. Some also have microphones built in to allow several people in on the conversation (though sometimes this makes it hard to hear on the other end). International calls, if kept short, are relatively inexpensive. The front of your phone directory gives complete information on placing international calls.

Pick a missionary that your church supports who
(1) is far away geographically,
(2) has easy access to a phone, and
(3) either lives in a time zone that would make a phone call during your group's regular meeting time convenient or would be willing to accommodate your group.

Write the missionary a letter to confirm a date and time that you will call. Also confirm the missionary's phone number. Once the number is confirmed, you might want to try calling on your own first to make sure everything is going to work okay. On the arranged night, gather the group around the phone. If they are unfamiliar with the missionary, tell them a bit about who he or she is and what the person does.

Then place the call. Let kids ask questions. Conclude the call by asking the missionary for prayer requests. Let him or her know that you will be praying about those things after you hang up; then conclude the call.

Ask kids: **How did it feel talking to someone that far away? How do you think it made that missionary feel?**

Point out how amazing technology allows us to communicate over such great distances. Remind kids that an even more amazing fact is that we can pray for people who live so far away and know that God hears and answers our prayers. Encourage kids to remember to pray for missionaries on a regular basis.

Conclude your time by praying together as a group for the requests your missionary gave you.

5. The Cast-Iron Styrofoam Cup

This idea works great when you're giving a devotional around a campfire. You might want to test it first, so you can time your remarks accordingly.

Fill a Styrofoam cup with water (it must be Styrofoam—not paper or plastic). As the kids watch carefully, set the cup into the fire, making sure it doesn't spill over. The kids will, of course, be waiting to see the cup melt and the water spill out. What they'll see though is an almost normal cup. The Styrofoam will melt down to the water line but then stop. You can actually boil water this way. The cup will eventually get so hot that the water will begin "sweating" out of it, at which point the cup will melt.

After allowing the kids to watch this for a while, ask them to explain why they think the cup doesn't melt. The reason is that the water in the cup dissipates the heat and keeps the cup from melting.

Have someone read II Corinthians 4:7.

Point out that non-Christians sometimes best understand God's power when they see a Christian depending on God during a difficult time and coming out stronger. Similarly, the miraculous thing about the cup in the fire was not just the strength of the cup, but the power of the water that allowed the cup to last longer than expected.

One of the keys to experiencing God's power in our lives is to be filled with the knowledge of God. The cup is only protected as far as it is filled. The more we understand who God is, how much He loves us, and what His will is for us, the better we will be able to withstand the pressures in our lives.

6. The Top Ten

To close a study on obedience or on the Ten Commandments, assign one commandment to each pair of kids. Have each pair compose a song that tells how to obey that command.

If you have less than twenty kids, omit some commands or let each pair choose a favorite command. Encourage kids to write peppy, memorable songs. Also encourage them to write about specific ways to obey the commandments.

Suggest that kids set their words to a contemporary tune, a commercial jingle, or a rap rhythm. A sample for "Remember the Sabbath day by keeping it holy" to the tune of "Row Your Boat" might be:

Rest, rest, rest Sunday,
Set the day apart,
It-is-good, re-fresh-ing, re-new-ing, en-rich-ing,
Imitate your Lord.

Invite pairs of volunteers to sing their songs for the group; then to lead the group in the song. If no one volunteers, lead the song yourself. Tell a funny tidbit about the composers, if you can.

Invite the group to identify the commandment each pair sings about.

Variation: Assign one of the following activities to each pair, and have them compose a list of ten commandments to govern that activity. After kids have shared the rules they came up with, point out that the commandments are usually designed to help us enjoy life more or to protect us, not to ruin our fun. The same is true of the Ten Commandments.

Assign activities such as golf, family vacations, succeeding in school, behaving at church, impressing someone of the opposite sex, Christmas shopping, being a friend, etc.

7. Ribbon Reminders

Pick a color that fits well with the theme you are trying to convey. Some examples might be green for moving on to maturity, white for remaining pure/holy, purple for God's presence with us wherever we go, or gray for overcoming and resisting temptation. The color and the theme should be closely intertwined and frequently repeated throughout the session. That way kids will associate the theme with the color after they leave.

Cuts strips of cloth (in that color) with a key verse written on them such as: " . . . God . . . will not let you be tempted beyond what you can bear. . . . he will also provide a way out so that you can stand up under it. (I Cor. 10:13)" or "Never will I leave you; never will I forsake you. (Heb. 13:5)"

Encourage kids to hang these strips in their lockers, in their cars, in their rooms, or wherever they need a reminder of the theme. Some may even choose to it on a tree limb in front of their school in order to be reminded of the truth each day as they go into the building. Others might tie it to their belt loops when they go on dates.

Variation: If you don't have the time or materials to write verses on the ribbons, just give them to your kids with nothing written on them. If you reinforce the connection between the color and the theme enough, the ribbons themselves will be a strong reminder of the message.

8. Accountability Partners

Many Christians struggle with keeping the daily disciplines of the Christian faith—Bible reading and prayer. One reason we so often neglect these disciplines is because no human watches us. Teachers await our homework and know if we don't do it. Bosses expect us to be at work and know if we don't come. Parents expect chores to be done and know if we neglect them. Church leaders expect us to fulfill what we've agreed to do at church. They know when we don't come or don't prepare. This human accountability helps us do what needs doing.

Encourage your kids to become accountable to each other so that they are more likely to pray and read their Bibles daily. Mix and match these possibilities as best fits the personality of your group:

• Have each kid give someone else in the group a wake-up call to remind him or her to allow time for God before school. Agree on times before calling and rotate calling responsibilities.

• Pair up and check with each other daily after school to confirm that each has completed five to ten minutes of Bible study and prayer.

• Pairs read the same passage and tell each other what they liked most about it.

• The whole group reads the same passage and takes a quiz on it. Those who pass earn a candy bar or other prize. Rotate quiz-writing responsibility among the group. Quiz makers get extra points for their efforts.

• Give points or single candies to those who read their Bibles five of the previous seven days. Assign groups and compete to add interest.

9. Manage Your Money

The Bible encourages us to give a tenth of our money and possessions to God (Mal. 3:10). As a result, many people think of that ten percent as God's money. In reality, *all* of our money belongs to God. We are the stewards and caretakers of money, not the owners. God is just as concerned with how we spend the ninety percent as He is with the ten percent we give to God.

Challenge kids to see all their money as belonging to God and to look to Him for help in spending it. Suggest they see their money as a way to make people happy, not as something to accumulate.

Give each person five pennies. Challenge kids to give all of their pennies away. The rules are:

(1) You must give one penny at a time.

(2) You cannot receive a penny at the same time you give one.

(3) You must accept every penny that is offered to you.

Debrief with questions like: **What happened? How did hoarding or hiding take away the fun of the game?**

How did breaking other rules impact the game?

What did you like about giving away your wealth?

What fears did you have?

How did the results confirm your fears or bring unexpected joy?

What happiness rules do people break in real life with money?

How can we make joy rather than give in to our fears?

What are ways to create joy with money without giving it away?

Point out that I Timothy 6:6-10 explains that money is potentially explosive, something we must handle with care and forethought. Hebrews 13:5 encourages us to depend on God for contentment, rather than on money. Challenge kids to search these two Scriptures for problems caused by loving money rather than using money for God's good.

Ask: **What grief does misuse of money bring?**

What are some ways to misuse money? (Hoard it; see it as the goal in life; buy a more-expensive item when a less-expensive item is sufficient; neglect human needs; spend exclusively on our pleasure; etc.)

What are some ways to use money for God's good? (Be honest about what is necessary and what is greed; budget so we can buy necessities; support a family; spend proportionately—some to meet other people's needs, some on food, some on clothing, some on housing, and so on; save for big purchases such as college, house, car, rather than taking out loans; find ways to stretch money as far as possible.)

At this point you probably aren't responsible for the food-clothing-and-shelter basics of life, but you still have money to spend. How can you know how much clothing and other possessions are enough?

Assure kids that we do need money—we need food, clothing, shelter, education—and that the way we manage this money can help us provide these necessities without hoarding, without being selfish, and without dishonoring God. Encourage teens to write what they need in life and how to manage their money to get there. Pause to ask God to guide this process.

Then focus on this year and this week with questions like: **What earning, spending, and saving goals do you think God wants for you in your life? This year? Right now?**

How will you spend your money this week in light of your lifetime goals?

Memorize I Timothy 6:6 by setting it to rhythm. Invite the group to seek contentment rather than cash, and to use their cash to help this contentment happen for them and those around them.

10. Cross-Cultural Community Challenge

Every youth group has its own cultural appeal, and this is often reflective of the culture of the parents or other adults in the church. The white, middle-class church tends to draw white, middle-class kids. But this closing challenge is designed to stir students to reach out beyond their normal cultural boundaries.

Invite a teacher or principal from a nearby school to speak with you at the close of a session on outreach. Ideally, this school leader should be from the school with the largest student representation in your youth group.

In an interview format, ask the school leader about the school in which he or she serves. Here are some sample questions you could ask:

What "cultures" are present in the school?

What "subcultures" exist as a result of differences in styles of dress, sports, intelligence, music, or ethnic background?

Where do these students live?

What are some of the challenges in their respective families?

Thank and dismiss your guest.

Then use Acts 1:8 to challenge your kids. Explain what it meant for those first Jewish believers to be told to reach out to "Samaria." Even though the Samaritans were geographically next door to the Jews, they were considered despised members of another culture. Being Christ's witnesses to our "Samaria" means reaching out to those who are geographically close, but culturally distant.

End the meeting by showing pictures of people or neighborhoods that represent some of the nearby cultures or subcultures that your youth group is not reaching. Ask:

Who is reaching these people? These neighborhoods? This "Samaria"?

11. So What?

One of the main questions you should be asking (in one form or another) at the close of each session is: **Now that you know it, what will you do about it?** Using a text related to putting faith into practice (like the faith/works teaching of James 2), close the meeting by challenging students to make an immediate application that they will share with the whole group.

Lead the way by showing students what you are asking them to do. Use a set statement (write it on a chalkboard, overhead transparency, or printed handout) such as:

"Since _____ (Scripture text) teaches me _____ (specific mandate), I have decided that this week I need to _____ (application)."

Make your own specific application or commitment, and share it with the group.

Examples might include, "Since <u>Matthew 5:43-48</u> teaches me <u>to love my enemies,</u> I have decided that this week I need to <u>be loving to one of my neighbors who I have been fighting with.</u>"

"Since <u>John 3:16</u> teaches me <u>that people who don't believe in Christ will die in their sin,</u> I have decided that this week I need to <u>witness to at least one person.</u>"

Have kids actually make a verbal commitment in front of their peers.

Note: You might want to tell kids at the beginning of the session what you want them to do so that they can think in advance about how they will respond.

12. Who's Gonna Reach 'Em?

After a discussion on outreach or witnessing, make a list of schools represented by the kids. (Try to get statistics from each school ahead of time on the total number of students that attend these schools.)

During the session, let kids estimate how many of these students might be Christians, and subtract that number from the total. This will leave you with the number of students yet to be reached for Christ— usually a very large number.

Write that number on the board, step back and say:

You know, it is not my job to reach these students. It is *your* job. My job is to prepare you to tell these students about Christ.

Have someone read Ephesians 4:11, 12 aloud, to back up your claim.

If you don't know how to reach these students, then I am not doing my job. But if I *am* doing my job and you aren't telling these kids about Christ, then *you* are dropping the ball.

Make sure you affirm any evangelistic efforts the kids are already making.

Conclude by asking several students representing various schools to pray that each Christian in the group, including the leader, will do his or her job.

13. Where's the Best Party?

The goal of this closing challenge is to help kids understand that following Jesus is a long-term commitment that does not always yield the maximum in short-term fun or immediate gratification.

Ask teens:

Would you like to have maximum fun? Would you like to live a wild and exciting life? Do you want to be at the center of the action?

Then surprise them by responding: **If you want to have maximum fun, then youth group is probably not your best bet.**

Explain that following Jesus involves lots of fun, joy, and happiness, but it also involves commitment, discipline, and obedience. Not everything we must do as followers of Christ will be fun or produce immediate happiness.

People who want maximum fun—at least for a short time— usually choose something other than following Jesus. Explain that sinful activities can be fun (that's why people do them!), but that they break down relationships.

• Getting drunk might be more fun than praying, but the former drives a wedge between us and God.

• Lying might be easier than telling the truth, but it creates a division between us and the people we lie to.

• Being selfish is more fun than serving others, but eventually people withdraw from a self-centered person who looks out only for himself.

Explain the nature of long-term fulfillment versus short-term "highs." Jesus promises long-term joy and satisfaction, whereas sinful activities usually provide only momentary fun.

If possible, conclude this meeting with a testimony from a Christian who formerly lived a wild, destructive life-style. Ask your guest to explain why he or she gave up the "fun" to follow Christ.

14. Bragging Rights

This concluding challenge could follow a discussion on heaven or heavenly rewards. It fits nicely after a study of the parable of the talents (Matt. 25:14-30).

Ask:

If you were given the opportunity to brag to Jesus about what you have done to honor and obey Him, what would you say? In other words, what faithful actions would you want Jesus to notice in your life?

Hand out pencils and paper so kids can write their answers down and keep them private. Encourage them to think in two categories. The first is the positive category. These are the positive things they've done that they would like Jesus to know about and affirm them for.

These actions might include "I witnessed to several of my friends," or "I reached out to a lonely student at school," or "I was loving and compassionate to my siblings and parents."

The second category includes negative actions that they didn't do as a result of following Jesus. These might include, "Because I committed myself to following You, I didn't cheat," or "I didn't give away my virginity," or "I didn't yield to the temptation to base my future decisions on monetary gain alone."

Point out that God already knows everything there is to know about us, and we don't need to "brag" to Him about our accomplishments. In fact, our good deeds or good behavior won't save us. We're only saved by God's grace through faith. However, these "bragging lists" could be used as reminders of what kids would like to be able to tell Christ on the day that He returns. Reassure kids that if they fail, Jesus is always ready to forgive them and give them a second (or third, or fourth . . .) chance.

15. Is Image Everything?

Ask: **Does anyone remember the commercial that aired not too long ago that claimed "Image is everything"? What do you think that statement means?** The kids will probably mention that in today's society, what we look like, the clothes we wear, the way we wear our hair, etc. seems to be what matters most to people.

Then ask: **If image is everything, what do you think it means when the Bible says that we are created in God's image?** Have someone read Genesis 1:27 and talk about what it means to be created in God's image.

When the Bible says that we are created in God's image, it doesn't mean that we were created to look exactly like Him physically. That would be impossible. Look at all the different kinds of people God created, with different colors of hair, different colors of eyes, different colors of skin. It sure looks as though God likes a lot of variety. We weren't all created to look exactly the same, and we don't all have to look exactly the same, no matter what society says.

When the Bible says we are created in God's image, it means that we were given His characteristics, like the abilities to love, think, and feel, and that we can become more and more like Him every day.

Do you think God is concerned about our image? Help kids to recognize that God wants us to become more like Him, so in that sense He does care about our "image," but not in the sense that society is concerned about our image.

God cares about what we look like on the inside, not what we look like on the outside.

Challenge your group to think about ways they can improve their image this week—the image that God wants them to have.

16. Pop Goes the Pop

Take your kids to an area of the church that's easy to clean, or take them outside to the parking lot. Have one of the youth leaders stand in front of the group, dressed as a teen and holding a can of pop.

Talk to the kids about the different pressures they face in a typical day. Encourage them to shout out situations they face that create pressure in their lives. (School, family, friends, etc.) As each pressure is called out, begin to shake the can of pop. Keep shaking the can until you've had a full, pressure-filled day, then crack open the pop can and let the contents spray.

When you've gotten the group back under control, talk about the fact that we are all under pressure every day and we can take a certain amount. When we reach our limit, however, and if we're pushed too far, we'll explode.

Have the kids brainstorm ways they can alleviate or avoid some of the pressures they face, and talk about things they can do when the pressure gets to be too much.

17. You've Got a Friend

Have kids list as many descriptions of Christ that they can think of. (Savior, Lord, healer, King of kings, all-powerful, Prince of peace, etc.)

Say: **The Bible tells us that we are to become imitators of God and Christ** (Ephesians 5:1, 2).

Does that mean that we're supposed to go out and get crucified? (Obviously, the answer to that one is no.)

Then what does it mean to be an imitator of Christ?

Talk about how Christ came to earth to be an example of how we can live our lives and how to treat other people, and that we can imitate Him by treating others as He did.

We can't be many of the things that Christ was. We can't be Savior, Lord, etc. But we can be a good friend to others. Christ was a good friend. What are some of the qualities Christ had that made Him a good friend?

Allow the kids time to think about this one and brainstorm a list of qualities that made Christ a good friend. Their list may look something like this:

- good listener
- very patient
- interested in me and my life
- willing to make sacrifices for me, etc.

When they've completed their list, talk about the qualities they've listed and why those qualities make someone a good friend.

Do you know anyone besides Christ who has all these qualities? If you don't have them all, does that mean you can't be a good friend? Talk about the fact that Christ was the only person who ever was, and the only person who ever will be, completely perfect. Because we haven't lived a perfect life, however, doesn't mean that we can't be a good friend to someone. We just won't ever be, nor will we ever find (other than Christ!) a perfect friend.

Challenge the group to think about the qualities they listed and how they can be a good friend to someone they know this week.

18. Oh, What Funnel

Hold up a funnel in front of your group. Have a variety of items next to you, and as you hold each one up, have the group try to guess whether or not it will fit through the funnel. Include both items that will and won't go through the funnel. Try things like marbles, dried beans, paper clips, peanuts, bananas, etc.

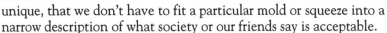

When you've gone through all the items, talk about how society is like a funnel and often tries to make us all fit a narrow description of who we should be. Then talk about the fact that God made each of us unique, that we don't have to fit a particular mold or squeeze into a narrow description of what society or our friends say is acceptable.

When we try to all squeeze into the same mold, a lot of us get stuck, just as many of the items got stuck or wouldn't fit through the funnel. Encourage kids to remember that God won't force us through a funnel, but recognizes and rejoices at our individuality.

19. Fast Break

Kids today hear a lot about the homeless and starving people in our world, so much so that many probably don't think about what it would be like to be really hungry. To help them gain a small understanding of what it is like, challenge them to fast for one day this week. You might even want to all choose the same day.

If kids haven't fasted before, you could challenge them to eat a hearty evening meal, and then eat nothing until the next evening meal. Be sensitive to those who might not be able to fast because of health reasons.

As they go through the day, have them keep track of their thoughts and feelings by jotting down notes at different times in the day. You could schedule a meeting on the evening of the day they fasted and share a very simple soup and bread supper to break the fast.

When kids return after fasting, ask them to bring in their notes and share a little of what it was like to go without food for a full day. Ask them to brainstorm ways they can help some hungry people (donating food to a local food pantry, supporting a hungry child through a Christian relief organization, living more simply, etc.).

Talk about why it is important to help people who are hungry (Matt.

25:31-46). Challenge them to choose one of the ways they listed, and help them see that they can make a difference in a hungry person's life.

20. Letter Rip

This idea can be used when talking about identifying with Christ or being known as a Christian. It can also be used in a more narrow sense when talking about the identification aspect of baptism.

Ask: **What physical things do people do to themselves to show that they are part of a certain group?**

After students give a few answers, say: **In many high schools, students who excel in sports are awarded letters that they sew on jackets (called letter jackets).**

Ask if any of your students have a letter jacket. If you have access to one, bring it in as an example.

Most schools that give letters only give them in sports. But some schools give letters for other areas of excellence. So you could be walking down the hall in one of these schools and see a student with a letter jacket for excellence in art, another for excellence in track, and another for excellence in math.

Then say: **Suppose your school (or this church) gave out letters for excellence in following Christ. How would you feel about wearing that letter jacket around your school? Would you wear it?**

If you got a letter in basketball, and one in following Christ, which would you be more proud of? Why?

What letters would be on your jacket? What would they stand for?

Have kids choose letters that have some special meaning for following Christ, and draw them in block letters like a letter jacket. Tape them on their backs as they leave the room.

Variation: Start by playing a game. Have kids write letters on sheets of paper and tape them to their backs with masking tape. Turn them loose to try to rip the letters off the others' backs. There are two ways to win: being the last person with a letter still on the back, or being the person who successfully collects the most letters from others' backs. After playing the game, discuss the above information.

21. Mediocrity Avoidance

Mediocrity is a big problem for today's Christian youth. Many teens want the benefits of Christianity without the costs—hence mediocrity.

Have your kids look at the following four passages. If you want to move through this more quickly, divide your class into four groups and assign one passage to each. If you have a little more time, have everyone work through all four passages.

Pass out blank pieces of paper and pencils or pens to each student. Then after each passage is read, have students write down what it means to them or how it applies to their lives.

The mediocrity avoidance passages are:
1. Revelation 3:15, 16
2. John 14:15
3. II Timothy 2:15
4. Romans 12:11

After you've worked through all four passages, have a few students share their thoughts.

Variation: Serve bland food (like lima beans, saltine crackers, or oatmeal) and a lukewarm beverage as you discuss the passages.

22. Human Love Meter

When you're talking about different types of love, give your students a tangible illustration with this visual idea.

Ask for five volunteers. When they come forward, give each one a sign to hold or wear around the neck. The signs should read:
1. Intellectual
2. Emotional
3. Social
4. Spiritual
5. Physical

Then explain that all dating relationships, in order to be healthy, need to have balance. Explain the five areas.

Intellectual means the level of knowledge the two have of each other. How much do they really know about each other?

Emotional refers to the amount of emotional involvement. How much do they "need" each other? Explain that this is often, but not always, much higher for girls than for guys.

Social means: How much fun do they have together? Are they friends? Do they enjoy each other's company?

Spiritual refers to the emphasis their relationship places on spiritual things. Do they talk about spiritual matters? Do they share their spiritual thoughts and questions? Do they pray together?

And *physical* of course, refers to their level of sexual involvement. This could be anywhere from holding hands to sexual intercourse.

Now tell the five volunteers you are going to describe the first dates of two couples and you want them to register the amount of intensity in each category. Once they're all standing in a line, explain that where they are presently standing is zero—nothing in that area. Tell them to move forward accordingly. Invite the students in the audience to suggest movements also.

Now describe two first dates, one at a time. Make the first couple very unbalanced. Describe how they both only talk about themselves, and end the date by making out in the back of the car. Make sure your "Human Love Meter" is adjusting.

Then describe the second couple. Make them a bit idealistic. They show genuine interest in each other, spend a few minutes in prayer together for her sick mother, and build no huge emotional ties. The guy could give the girl a good night kiss on the hand. Kids should adjust their meters accordingly.

If you have time, let some kids compose other first-date scenarios and have the "Human Love Meter" adjust to them as well.

Then ask your teens about unbalanced relationships. Ask them what happens when a relationship has a high emotional intensity and nothing else. Ask them what happens when a relationship has a high physical intensity and nothing else, and so on.

23. Sheep and Goats

Matthew 25:31-46 is a powerful passage on serving. Help your teens apply the passage by making reference to two levels of meaning—literal and metaphorical. Make sure kids understand what these mean before you dive in.

Say: **If someone is standing in the middle of a field and a large cow is charging toward that person, and he/she says, "She's a big cow!"— that's referring to the cow on a literal level. But if that same person were standing in the middle of gym class and points to a girl across the room and says, "She's a big cow!"—that would be speaking on a metaphorical level. It would also be rude.**

In the same sense, we can apply this passage by looking at both the literal meaning, as well as a metaphorical parallel to our world.

Have kids identify the six types of needy people referred to in Matthew 25:31-46. They're listed four times (hungry, thirsty, stranger, naked, sick, in prison)!

Now work through these one at a time, applying them literally, and with the metaphorical definitions below. As you discuss each category, have your students identify (on a piece of paper) someone they know who fits that description.

Hungry—someone whose basic needs aren't being met (love, affection, affirmation, sense of worth).

Thirsty—emotionally dried out (like a dry sponge—even if you put a little water in it, you still can't squeeze any out).

Stranger—alone, outsider (can be very well known, and still be an outsider).

Naked—exposed (everyone can see the person's problems and needs).

Sick—something beyond their control is keeping them from being whole (divorce, death of a loved one, abuse, dumped by a girlfriend/boyfriend).

In Prison—trapped by something of their own doing (drugs, alcohol, lying, gossip, sexual looseness).

After your students have identified someone in each category, have them circle one person on their sheets who they will try to help.

24. Pew Potatoes

Here's a study that your students are sure to eagerly consume. When talking about television (choices, effects, etc.), tape three 10-minute segments of popular shows. Then watch them together as a class. Hand out paper and pencils to your students and tell them to take notes on two things:

1. Characters and situations that obviously go against biblical teaching; instances of sin.

2. Positive moral values or actions, if any.

After viewing, get feedback from your group as to their findings. Compare the "negative" list with the "positive" list.

25. Hope Springs Eternal

A great way to address the topic of hope is to look at some of the assurances we have according to the Bible.

Salvation—Have your students read I John 5:11-12.

Then ask: **If you have Christ, what do you have?** (Salvation.)

If you don't have Christ, what do you have? Let kids speculate about what they think heaven and hell might be like.

Answered Prayer—Have your students read John 16:24.

Ask: **What prayer of yours has God answered?**

What do you wish you had prayed about?

What things should you be talking to God about?

Victory over Sin—Read I Corinthians 10:13.

Then ask: **What are some temptations that teens struggle with?**

What are some temptations that are hard for you to fight?

How do you feel when you beat Satan's temptations?

What's a good game plan for being victorious over a recurring temptation?

Forgiveness—Read I John 1:9. Then ask your students to give examples of a time they forgave someone.

Next ask: **Do you really believe God has forgiven and forgotten your old sins?**

How do your actions and attitudes reflect your answer to this question?

Guidance—Have your students read Proverbs 3:5, 6. Ask kids to list areas teens have a hard time entrusting to God.

Then ask: **Is there anything you wish you'd trusted God about that you didn't at the time?**

In what areas do you need guidance right now?

Have your group spend a minute in silent prayer, asking for God's guidance in one specific area.

26. Rip Torn

Here's one way to demonstrate the long-term nature of sexual relationships.

Start by taking two different colored pieces of construction paper. Glue them together. (You might want to glue them together in advance, so the glue is dry). As you let the glue dry, point out that this is like people who bond together in an intimate sexual relationship.

After the glue is dry, have a student try to separate the two pieces. Assuming you used lots of glue, and that it dried, it should be nearly impossible to cleanly separate the two pieces of paper. Each one should tear some, and leave bits and pieces on the other.

Repeat the process several times adding other pieces of paper to one of the original pieces. Point out how each time, the paper gives something of itself. In the same way, the sexual union between two people was intended to be permanent, and within the confines of monogamous marriage. When it's not, something is lost each time.

We can certainly be forgiven for past sexual sins, but the consequences might have long-term ramifications. Give each kid a piece of the tattered paper as he/she leaves.

27. Heir-a-parent

Have someone read aloud Ephesians 6:1-3.

Ask: **Why is it sometimes hard to obey your parents?**

If no one mentions it, suggest that not understanding their motives—

why they want you to do or not do something—can make it hard to do what they say.

When you're reading a book or watching a movie, what things determine how much you enjoy it?

If no one mentions it, suggest that identifying with a particular character is an important factor.

Identifying with a character involves seeing things from that person's perspective and understanding why he or she acts and feels the way he or she does. The more you identify with a character, the more you will probably enjoy the book or movie.

The same principle could also be applied to your relationship with your parents. The more you try to identify with them, the more you will probably "enjoy" your relationship with them.

When you're given a rule or curfew that seems unreasonable, what is usually your first reaction? If you're like most of us, your first reaction is probably to argue or complain.

But what if, instead of arguing or complaining, your first reaction was to stop and consider *why* your parents created this rule or curfew? Try to identify with what they're feeling. Are they worried about what might happen to you? Are they reacting to a past bad experience, perhaps a time when you violated their trust? Are they struggling with the idea of giving you more freedom?

Chances are, if you're trying to identify with your parents' feelings, you may find that their biggest motivation is concern for you. If you recognize that, you'll probably be better able to obey their rules and curfews—as Ephesians 6:1 instructs. You may also be better able to communicate with them about the rules and curfews that you think are unfair or extreme.

Which of the following responses do you think would lead to better communication with your parents?

(a) "That's not fair!"

(b) "I know that you gave me this rule because you don't want me to get into trouble—and I appreciate that. But maybe there's another way we can make sure I stay out of trouble."

Variation: Ask kids to come to the meeting dressed like one of their parents. Tell them to raid their parents' closets. Make sure you warn parents about this in advance. To make the point even more memorable, invite parents to the meeting dressed like their kids! Discuss the need to identify with each other.

28. Map It Out

Get a map of your local area. Stick pins in the locations where your kids live. Connect the pins with strings to show your group's "sphere of influence" in your area. Encourage kids to begin to make a difference in that "sphere of influence." This may involve anything from just being friendlier to the people in that area (saying hello on the street) to organizing a food or clothing drive for the needy in the area.

Variation: Show on a world map where kids have traveled to demonstrate the potential for worldwide influence we have.

Take-Action Steps

1. Traveling Evangelists

Let students do more than just hear a message on taking the Gospel to those who haven't heard. Let them actually take the message to those who haven't heard.

Make a tape recording of the morning sermon and duplicate enough tapes to give to everyone on the church's roster who hasn't attended church in the past two months. (If the pastor knew ahead of time what the group was doing, an appropriate sermon could be prepared accordingly.)

Designate roles for all participants based on their gifts and interests, such as: recording engineer, navigator, driver, doorbell ringer, greeter, etc. Obtain a list of names and addresses from the church secretary and hit the streets taking the Gospel to those who might not have heard it lately. Many will appreciate your concern, as well as the tape, and might even show up for worship the next Sunday.

You might find out that some are attending another church and this information would be helpful for those in charge of church records. Others may have been ill or discouraged and students would get hands-on experience in real-life ministry.

Variation: Tape a talk you've given to the youth group. Include some personal greetings and/or words from some of the kids in your group. Make copies of the tape and take it to those on the youth group mailing list who haven't been there in a while. As you go house to house, discuss what it would be like to take the Gospel to someone in another land.

2. In-House Outreach

Rather than simply encouraging teens to go out and involve their friends in church, start the process during your meeting. Show them how to do outreach by doing it together. Possibilities include:

• Distribute postcards and lists of names and addresses of local teens and occasional visitors. Have kids write a welcome postcard to kids on the list. You can write some sample phrases on the chalkboard to help kids a little with what to say, but encourage them to use their own words and to customize each card.

Here is a sample of what kids could write to someone who hasn't shown up lately:

> *Hi! We've missed seeing you around lately. Your smile and good ideas always make our group better. Can you come to our next Bible study? It's this Wednesday night. Call if you need a ride.*

For someone who has *never* come, kids could write:

> *Hi! I'm Corey and I'm a member of ___ church. I'd love for you to get to know the people in our group. We have Bible studies every Wednesday that are casual and interesting . . .*

• Bring in a supply of small milk cartons that are empty and clean. On one of the side panels, have kids write: "Missing" and then glue on a picture or a drawing of a group member who hasn't been around much lately. Inside the carton they could write a short note like this:

> *Don't be a missing person! Come join us at our pizza party Friday, April 24 at 7:00. Call if you need a ride.*

• If your church has multiple phone lines, put a few kids at each phone to call kids who aren't there. Having several conversations going on at once adds to the fun. Let kids call unchurched friends as well as those they haven't yet met. Practice how to make phone calls to new friends.

• Wrap a series of presents for a fellow teen who is hospitalized or going through a crisis. Consider taking at least one or two kids along ahead of time to shop for these. Let kids wrap the gifts and add personal notes. The notes can be bundled separately or attached to presents to be opened one-a-day. Take the whole group or selected volunteers along to deliver the gifts, obeying visitor guidelines.

3. Who You Gonna Call?

Here's another way to reach out to "fringe" group members. After a discussion or a Bible study on Christian fellowship or even the "lost sheep" of Luke 15, group members often realize that certain kids have dropped out from the group. The question is, "How can we reach out to these kids? How can we go out in search of the 'lost sheep' from our group?"

This "take action" challenge launches students right into the outreach. After expressing concern for teens who seemed to have dropped out, give each group member a list of names (at least two but no more than five) and explain that you are all going to engage in "Operation Phone Barrage," an aggressive program to find out where inactive students have gone.

Instruct kids before sending them off. Give them basic lines of introduction—who they are, where they are from, and why they are calling. To ease the awkwardness of calls like these, a phone-calling outreach works best if students include in their calls an invitation to a specific activity—a retreat, concert, or other big event.

Then, after a prayer together, send kids off—either to the church phones (ideally) or a phone bank at a nearby shopping center (not ideal, but often the only option; note: if this is the option you pursue, bring plenty of change!).

Your kids may find out that students have moved, changed churches, or simply decided to drop out of church, but almost everyone will find at least one "lost sheep" who was glad to receive the call and who will consider returning to the youth group.

4. Mobile Car Wash

In a lesson on outreach you might point out the tendency we have to expect non-Christians to take the initiative and come to our church or a big concert or youth rally. It's exciting to do big things and it seems a lot easier and less scary than trying to go meet people individually. Yet the sad truth is that many of the people who need it most never show up.

You might draw the analogy of a fund-raising car wash. Many youth groups host car washes to attract lots of people in order to raise money. Yet there are still lots of people with dirty cars who never come. What if you took the car wash to them? Load kids up in cars with adult sponsors. Make sure each car has a hose, buckets, soap, sponges, and towels. The goal is to go to people's houses and offer to wash their cars for free. The contest is to see which group can get the most cars done in an hour.

The leader's job is to make sure people understand that this is a valid church activity and that the kids do a good job. After the groups return, you could discuss the similarities kids see between this and trying to share with people how Jesus can wash away their sins. (Some people won't be interested even though they need it. Some won't trust you. Some will tolerate you. Some will be very glad you came.)

5. Put Your Money Where Your Mouth Is

After a lesson on the tongue, challenge kids to pick a negative speech pattern that they want to work on. It might be something like put-downs, or using the word "god" as a slang expression, or gossiping. If you want, have kids write their speech-improvement goals on wooden tongue depressors. Have kids keep track of each other over the next week (or longer). Every time one of them catches himself (or someone else) in the act, the offender has to agree to bring a nickel for each offense to the next meeting.

The money you collect could be sent as a gift to the student body fund of a rival high school. If you have more than one school represented in your group, collect the money from each school and send it to one of the others. The reason for doing this as opposed to giving it to a missionary or other worthy cause is because you don't want the result of negative speech to be seen as a positive contribution. You want to drive home the point that foolish speech really works against oneself.

6. Church Chat

After a session on the church and our place within it, have kids brainstorm a list of five specific things they could do right now to serve your church. The list might include things such as:
- staffing the infant nursery during a worship service or special program
  - pulling weeds out of the church flower beds
  - washing windows in the Sunday school classrooms
  - greeting visitors on Sunday morning
  - ushering
  - reading Scripture during a worship service
  - teaching children's church
  - visiting shut-ins, etc.

When you have your list, tell kids that between them all, they have to do these five items within some time frame you set (perhaps two or three weeks). Have them form task forces to accomplish each item. Plan some type or party to reward them after all the jobs are done.

7. Billboard

When studying life's injustices, the reliability of God's promises, and the agony of waiting for evil to be wiped out once and for all, focus on Habakkuk 2:2-4.

God instructed Habakkuk to write down God's revelation, the fact that good will win out, that God's ways really do work, and that good guys may finish last, but they will certainly finish. The tablet on which Habakkuk wrote was meant for many people to see, perhaps fulfilling the same purpose as a present day billboard. It was a tangible reminder of God's truth and God's care.

Let kids make their own billboard, perhaps quoting Habakkuk 2:3, 4, or perhaps quoting another Bible truth they want people to see and live. Mount the billboard in the youth hall, in another pre-approved location inside or outside the church, or consider renting a billboard in your community.

The billboard can be of paper, poster board, canvas, wood, or whatever material is available and appropriate for your purpose. A billboard to be placed inside the church for a single week does not need to be as durable as one you'll mount outside for a month.

Let the truths that are expressed be those that people who don't have a church background can understand. You might want to clear this with the church board, or other governing body, especially if you intend to display your billboard outside the church.

8. TV Ratings

In the newspaper every week you can find a listing of the top television shows. Cut this out and bring it to your class.

Explain: **In order to get this information, companies enlist the help of thousands of families across the United States. These families keep a diary or a log of everything they watch. Then the information from these diaries is compiled into a report each week. We're going to do our own little survey.**

Pass out copies of a page that has the days of the week written down the left side. Instruct your students to keep a log of everything they watch during that week.

When you gather the next week, some students won't have kept the log. So have extra copies and instruct them to think back over the week and write down what they watched. Have a couple TV listings available to help them remember.

Compile the information together as a group and post the "ratings" for your group. Compare your ratings with the national ratings.

Ask: **Most studies show that people who call themselves Christians watch the same shows as everyone else. Do you think there should be a difference? Why or why not?**

Continue to talk about how to make choices in TV watching. You could extend this activity for several weeks, challenging kids to evaluate their viewing choices before, during, and after they watch a particular show.

9. TV Chide

Kids know that lots of people complain about how much violence there is on TV, but most don't think that they can do anything about it. Have each member of your group write a letter to your local TV station (or to a network if they'd rather), naming shows he or she is opposed to and why. Ask the station (or network) to remove that program from the air.

Though their letters alone may not change what network executives decide to air on TV, help the kids see that there are steps they can take to positively influence society. If enough concerned people take positive action, it can make a big difference.

10. Seniors Fair

We all know that there is a wealth of wisdom and love kids can receive by connecting with older members of your congregation. After a lesson on respecting and learning from our elders, plan a Seniors Fair. Many of the older adults in your church have led very interesting lives. They have had unique careers, hobbies, and experiences. Often teens don't even realize what interesting things these "old" people do and have done.

Go to your seniors group and invite them to come and share their hobbies and experiences with your group. Set up a room with tables where senior adults can display items demonstrating their interests. Create the atmosphere of a fair with refreshments, decorations, and some games. Invite the youth to come and see the displays. Use some adult sponsors to help kids move around to all the different displays and ask questions. The goal is to get kids talking to a generation they too easily forget.

11. Friendships with the Wise

Here's another idea for spending time with older adults. Study passages like II Timothy 1:3-7, Proverbs 16:31, and Proverbs 2—4. These are passages that highlight the value of letting those who have already been there teach us how to live our faith. Then take action that will lead to relationships with elders.

Survey one or more senior adult classes for adults who are willing to partner with a young person for three months of friendship and encouragement. Survey kids for those willing to partner with an adult. With the help of the teachers of the adult classes, match kids with adults by personality and other factors. Gather partners for an idea-generating meeting. Ask: **What kind of relationship would you like to develop with your partner? How could you get to know each other better?** List ideas such as:

- Send each other cards or letters once a month.
- Interview each other about what it's like to be an adult/youth.
- Request prayer from each other, and pray for each other's requests.
- Call each other once a week to tell what's happening.
- Sit in church together at least once during the three-month match.
- Eat a meal in each other's home, here at church, or in a restaurant.
- Youth tell adults what kids want adults to know about kids. Adults tell youth what adults want kids to know about adults.
- Share favorite Bible verses with one another.

Perhaps you'll compose and duplicate for each partner a calendar suggesting one of these actions a week.

At the close of the three months, evaluate how to make this process even better. Begin another three-month match. Don't be surprised if friendships continue.

Hint: As you make matches, don't rule out shut-ins who are unable to come to church or to meetings. Phone calls, letters, and youth-initiated visits are still possible and profitable.

12. Try It for a Month

If you have a session on obedience, encourage kids to focus on an area of obedience for one month—a very manageable amount of time. Focus on a life-style change called for in the Bible passage you're studying. Identify advantages associated with that change. Give as much attention to "things to do" as to "things not to do" that will bring about that change. Encourage kids to motivate each other and to hold each other accountable. After the month is up, evaluate what's easy and hard about the new life-style pattern. Focus on what's good about the change, even though it's hard. Then name reasons to keep up the habit. Point out that God wants obedience. As we obey a day at a time, we can find lifelong joy.

Certain challenges will be easier for some kids than for others. Rather than promoting pharisaical attitudes, challenge kids to encourage and commend each other on their decisions and follow through. Where applicable, participate in some of the life-style changes yourself.

Sample life-style changes might include:

- I'll use words that build up rather than tear down, so all of us can feel more loved (Eph. 4:29).

• I'll listen to more Christian music. This will help me think more about God and can strengthen my faith (Rom. 12:1, 2). Or, I'll stop listening to a certain type of music or radio station.

• I'll repeat no gossip, no matter how juicy. If I have to say something about someone, it will be a complement. I hope this will encourage people to see the best in each other (Eph. 4:31).

• I'll watch one hour or less of television daily to allow me more time for other things (Eph. 5:15, 16). Or, I'll only watch two shows each week.

• I'll read my Bible at least five minutes a day so I can know how to obey God (Eph. 5:10).

• I'll drink no alcohol so I can focus on life (Luke 1:15).

• I'll stop doing _____ . Let kids make a vague or unnamed commitment like this, especially if it's a sexual behavior (Heb. 13:4).

13. Accent-uate the Positive

If you've been talking about world missions, conclude by challenging your kids to befriend people from other ethnic groups—people in their schools or neighborhoods.

Offer a brief international training course for students.

Say: **Start simply by getting to know people. Ask them about their country** (encourage students to look these countries up on a map). **Eventually, see if you can get them to talk about their religious perspective. What religion are they? What do they believe? How have their beliefs affected them here?**

In the midst of this learning experience, tell kids to avoid two common mistakes that Westerners often make with people from other ethnic groups.

First, be patient with their accents. When it is difficult or almost impossible to communicate, don't stop trying. For example, if you are trying to communicate with a Hispanic neighbor who doesn't know much English, occasionally ask a friend who is studying Spanish to try to interpret for you. Speak slowly and clearly. If they know a little English, speaking slowly will give them time to translate words in their heads.

Second, avoid the temptation to try to explain all of the Gospel in the first conversation. Some people have never heard about Jesus. Others come from ancient cultures and religions, so they will be less open to the message of Christ. Develop friendships first; then explain the Gospel as the friendship grows.

Always follow up on kids' progress during future sessions.

If you get permission, focus on patients who don't receive many visitors. Pair up small teams of kids with an adult leader who can model this ministry for them and train them.

You might want to provide large group basic training on visitation. Teach kids how to ask good questions, read appropriate Scriptures, or pray with those they are visiting. Teach them that there is value is quietly visiting. Advise students of the importance of "just sitting" with patients—even if nothing is said.

The "take action" challenge might also include testimonies from several students who have actually done such a visit with you—so that other students can gain confidence to join in the outreach.

14. Single-Parent Relief Force

Single parents (often moms) are frequently faced with insurmountable challenges in caring for their households and families. One "take action" challenge in response to this need is to give students a chance to respond by committing themselves to some practical action for the week ahead.

A leader from the church's single-parent ministry could come to the youth group and present a variety of needs. If your church doesn't have an organized single-parent ministry, then invite a single parent to come and talk about his or her needs. Then kids could break into groups by interest and/or skill area and decide how they are going to respond.

Here are examples of groups kids could participate in:

• *Leaf it to me*—kids who commit to raking the yard of one or several single-parent households.

• *Operation oil slick*—mechanically oriented group members who offer to spend a Saturday morning changing the oil in single moms' cars—free of charge.

• *No charge baby-sitting*—kids who volunteer a certain number of hours per week or month, which will be donated to help single parents get out of the house for a while.

• *Saturday morning out*—single parents drop their kids off at church for a Saturday morning of fun and games organized by your group. This works especially well around Christmas, as the parents will appreciate the chance to do some shopping without the kids.

• *You pay/We shop*—kids (with access to a car) who volunteer to spend an hour or so each week doing the needed food-shopping for some single parent (who provides the list and the money).

Obviously, the greatest challenge will be implementing the tasks for which kids volunteer, but it is a "take action" item which allows kids to meet a tangible need within the church family.

15. Giving Forgiveness

At the conclusion of a session on forgiving others, exhort kids to take action—either to go and seek forgiveness from people whom they have wronged or to grant forgiveness to people who have wronged them.

Explain that forgiveness is a two-way street; however, the Bible teaches that we are responsible to act in forgiving ways. If we have committed a sin, we need to ask forgiveness, like Zacchaeus. Luke 19 says that when Zacchaeus realized the way that he had cheated people, that he promised to pay them back—up to four times what he had taken from them.

If someone has sinned against us, we likewise need to take action. According to Matthew 18, we need to confront him or her in hopes of bringing that person to genuine repentance. But, according to Ephesians 4:32, we need to forgive that person from the heart no matter what the response.

After teaching about forgiveness, hand out three-by-five cards on which kids will record their intended courses of action.

Say: **Ask yourselves: Is there someone from whom I need to ask forgiveness?**

How will I go and seek forgiveness and restoration?

Is there someone who has sinned against me whom I need either to confront or forgive from my heart?

Close the meeting in quiet prayer where group members can commit their action to God and—if necessary—seek the forgiveness of others in the group.

16. Visiting the Unvisited

This exercise can build and demonstrate compassion. It will work best at the conclusion of a session on a text such as Matthew 25:31-46—"I was sick, and you looked after me" (Matt. 25:36) or James 1:27 about visiting widows and orphans.

The call to action will function most effectively if the youth group can respond immediately with a visitation program of some sort, although it will work if the call to action at the close of the meeting includes some definite commitment by students to do visitation.

The "take action" challenge reflects Jesus' special concern for the lonely, the deserted, and the isolated. Challenge teens to join you on a visit to a hospital, nursing home, or long-term care facility. You will have to get special permission from facility administrators to do this. (Permission is not necessarily always easy to get if your church is not already operating a program there.)

17. Friend Ship-Shape

After a session on friendship, have kids brainstorm qualities that make someone a good friend. Write these ideas down on a large sheet of paper. Then give each member of your group seven cards (3 x 5 index cards would work well) and have them write "A friend loves at all times, Proverbs 17:17" across the top of each card, and list one quality of a good friend on each card.

Challenge them to pick one card per day throughout the following week and try to show the friendship quality listed on that card that day. At the end of the day, they can write on the card how they showed that trait and to whom. Encourage them to remember that no matter which trait they are showing, love is behind each one.

18. Idol Sale

When the apostle Paul preached the Gospel in Ephesus, some people responded in this way: "A number who had practiced sorcery brought their scrolls together and burned them publicly. When they calculated the value of the scrolls, the total came to fifty thousand drachmas" (Acts 19:19).

Combine a fun event with a meaningful session on idolatry. After the session, give students one hour to go home and raid their rooms of any items that have become idols for them; posters, tapes, sports paraphernalia, cosmetic non-essentials, maybe some will even have occult items. While the students are gathering items, set up a spontaneous garage sale on tables in front of the church. If you don't think a spontaneous sale will work, collect items over several weeks, and publicize the sale. Let students donate other items they don't need, even if they aren't necessarily idols.

If your church wouldn't want items to be sold on the church grounds, hold the sale somewhere else. When kids return, have them sell their "idols" and donate the money to the youth group's efforts to reach students for Christ. Weed through the items to make sure nothing is offensive or in poor taste. If you do collect any occult items, it's better to throw them away than to sell them.

Use the money to provide one scholarship for an upcoming retreat or camp. Or buy extra Bibles for use by the group.

19. Idol Burning

Here's another activity related to idols.

You'll need a large container of water. If you have a small class, this container could be a good-sized wastebasket. But if you have more than twenty kids, you should probably use a large trash can or barrel. Make sure the water isn't going to leak out! Fill the container with water and place it outside near your room.

Teach your kids about idols using the Book of Hosea. This is a fascinating story of God's anger over the Israelites' continuous rejection of Him and His persistent love for them. You could also point out that the purchasing of Gomer is a foreshadowing of Christ's redemptive work on our behalf.

Then have your group brainstorm a list of possible "idols" of teens today. Make the list as long as you can. You might even make this a competition by dividing your class into two teams and seeing which team can come up with more idols.

After your list is done, pass out pieces of paper to each student. Have all of them write "My personal Idol" across the top of the page. Next have kids draw a picture of what an idol might have looked like back in Hosea's time, leaving room inside the idol to write. Now have your students write a word or phrase or draw a symbol inside the idol that represents an idol in their lives. Define the word idol. (You could say that an idol is something that they value more than their relationship with God or something that damages their relationship with God.)

Take your group to the container of water. Explain that this is not a time for goofing around. Do not tolerate any acting up or the experience will be ruined for everyone—and could become unsafe!

Have your kids pray silently, asking for forgiveness for putting things before Him. Then, as a symbol of their desire to put Christ first in their lives, have your students come up one or two at a time and set their papers on fire. Make sure they are holding them directly over the container of water. They can hold on to the paper momentarily while it burns. Then they should drop the paper into the water and return quietly to where they were standing.

Variation: Instead of the container of water, add the idols to a bonfire. This might be safer. It would be a great closing activity for a camp-out or retreat.

20. Helping the Homeless

One of the big problems in today's society, as most of your kids will know, is the plight of homeless people. To help your kids see that they can make a difference in the lives of these people, over a period of several weeks, have them bring things from their *own* closets for a garage sale or donation to a homeless shelter. You can also invite other area youth groups to participate.

The proceeds from the sale (or the clothes themselves) can be donated to a local shelter for the homeless.

If there's a homeless shelter or a soup kitchen close by, arrange to have your group staff it for a certain evening. This could become a monthly commitment. You'll always want to send at least one adult volunteer with any kids who participate in a ministry like this.

21. Pet Project

After a lesson on caring for *all* of God's creation, have a pet-food drive and donate the food to your local animal shelter. (Call the shelter first to see what their needs are, and let kids know what is needed as you begin to collect donations.) You might also be able to arrange a visit to the animal shelter so your kids can see firsthand what goes on there. Some shelters are looking for volunteers to come and play with various animals on a regular basis. After expressing your care in some way, point out that while it's important to care for animals, we need to show even more compassion to people.

22. Garbage Collectors

After a session on being responsible stewards of God's world, have kids collect all the garbage they would normally throw away during the week in a garbage bag (or bags!). Make sure they know that this is *their* garbage only, not their friends' or family's.

The following week, have the kids bring their garbage and put it all together to see how much the group as a whole collected. Seeing just how much garbage they produce in a week could make quite an impact. You might even want to weigh the garbage and calculate how much trash the group probably throws away in a year.

Talk about ways the kids can reduce their *own* garbage output, and help them see that even one person can make a difference.

Variation: Divide into teams. Assign each team an adult volunteer. Give each team several plastic garbage bags. Have a contest to see which team can fill the most bags with litter they find on the ground. (The adult volunteers are to make sure that groups don't try to cheat by filling up bags with litter that isn't on the ground or with rocks or tree limbs or hubcaps or . . .) Depending on how much time you have, give the teams 30-45 minutes to work.

Seeing how much litter they collect in such a short time should give kids a better idea of how important environmental issues are and how little time it can take to make difference.

23. Worship Dissection

After teaching on worship, get a copy of an "order of service" from your church and copy it for your students or make an overhead transparency of it. Most churches type these up weekly for the pastor's reference. If your church doesn't have one of these, you have two other options:

(1) if your church bulletin has a fairly detailed outline of the service, that will work just fine; or

(2) bite the bullet and actually write it out!

With your class, go over the components of your church's worship service one item at a time deciding how each aspect lends itself to worship (or doesn't).

Then have your class put their learning into practice by designing a worship service. This can take one of four routes, and you'll need to decide beforehand which you're using.

1. Design a worship service for the whole church if your pastor will let you. Then have the students involved in leading the service.

2. Design a short worship service for your class and "do" it right then.

3. Design a worship service for younger children.

4. Design a worship service for a nursing home.

Try to get your students thinking about fresh ways to worship God, not just including the same old components of worship you've always had.

24. Top Forty

For a session on music, have kids bring in their entire music collections in a box (or a truck). During the session, have kids make a list of ways to evaluate music, taking into account the lyrics, the lifestyle of the artists, etc.

At the close of the session, have kids develop two top-twenty lists: the twenty best songs; and the twenty worst songs. Don't simply lump all Christian music into the best category and all secular music into the worst category. In fact, you might want to limit the activity to secular music only.

Challenge kids to dig deeper. Let them determine what makes a song fit into the "best" or "worst" category, but challenge them to focus on the message of the songs, and how the message fits with a Christian worldview. In fact, you might want to limit the activity to secular music only.

Have a boombox or two on hand (capable of playing cassettes and CDs) to help kids as they evaluate the songs that don't have lyrics included.

25. Book Reviews

Kids are used to giving book reports in school, but maybe they've never had to give one at church. After a session on studying the Bible, or the importance of reading Scripture, assign each kid a book of the Bible to read and report on. It might add an element of fun if you put several book names into a container and have kids choose which ones they have to read. Consider dividing some of the longer books into shorter sections.

Ask that the book reports be in the students' own words, not simply copied from the text notes of a study Bible. Encourage kids to type them, too. Two to three pages should be sufficient. You could give them a simple outline to follow:
1. Title of book
2. About the author
3. What it's about (main theme)
4. What I liked best
5. What I didn't understand
6. What I learned

Have kids treat this like they would a school assignment. During your next session, have kids share their reports. Be prepared to ask them some questions about each book.

Variation: Extend the idea to include other Christian books you think your kids should read. Develop a point system and award kids who collect a certain number of points during the year. You could plan a special party just for these kids.

26. 3:16

John 3:16 is probably one of the most memorized verses in the Bible. After stressing the importance of Bible memory, divide into groups and see which group can memorize the most other 3:16 verses in the Bible within the next twenty minutes. Some of the verses will be obscure (like Deut. 3:16 and II Chron. 3:16); some will be easy to memorize (like I

Kings 3:16 and Romans 3:16); and some will be well worth memorizing (like Luke 3:16; I Cor. 3:16; Col. 3:16; II Tim. 3:16; James 3:16; and Rev. 3:16).

Variations: (1) Form teams and have each team choose another meaningful 3:16 verse in the Bible and illustrate it in some way.

(2) Have kids list all the things we'd learn about in the Bible and God if all we ever had were the 3:16 verses.